CISTERCIAN FATHERS SERIES: NUMBER EIGHTEEN

Bernard of Clairvaux
Amadeus of Lausanne

MAGNIFICAT

CISTERCIAN FATHERS SERIES: NUMBER EIGHTEEN

MAGNIFICAT

HOMILIES IN PRAISE OF THE BLESSED VIRGIN MARY

by

Bernard of Clairvaux
and
Amadeus of Lausanne

Translated by
MARIE-BERNARD SAÏD
and
GRACE PERIGO

Introduction by CHRYSOGONUS WADDELL ocso

§

CISTERCIAN PUBLICATIONS INC.
Kalamazoo, Michigan
1979

CISTERCIAN FATHERS SERIES

BOARD OF EDITORS

A translation from the Latin of *Homilia in laudibus virginis matris* by Bernard of Clairvaux from the critical edition by Jean Leclercq and H. Rochais, *Sancti Bernardi Opera, IV* (Rome: Editiones cistercienses, 1966) 13-58, and of *Homiliae octo felicis memoriae Amedei episcopi Lausannensis de laudibus beatae Mariae* from the critical edition of G. Bavaud, *Amédée de Lausanne: Huit Homélies Mariales*, Sources chrétiennes, 72 (Paris: Editions du Cerf, 1960).

Bernard of Clairvaux (1090–1153)
Amadeus of Lausanne (1110–1159)

© Cistercian Publications, Inc., 1979

Available in the Commonwealth and Europe through
A. R. Mowbray and Co. Ltd, St Thomas House
Becket Street, Oxford OX1 1SJ

Library of Congress Cataloging in Publication Data

Main entry under title:

Magnificat.

(Cistercian Fathers series ; no. 18)
"A translation from the Latin of Sermones in laudibus Beatae Virginis Matris, by Bernard of Clairvaux (1090-1153), and Homiliae octo Amedei Episcopi Lausannensis Beatae Mariae, of Amadeus of Lausanne (1110-1159)."
Includes index.
1. Mary, Virgin—Sermons. 2. Sermons, English —Translations from Latin. 3. Sermons, Latin— Translations into English. I. Bernard de Clairvaux, Saint, 1091?-1153. II. Amadeus, Saint, Bp. of Lausanne, 1110 (ca.)–1159.
BT608.A1M33   232.91   78-6249
ISBN 0-87907-118-4

Book design by Gale Akins at Humble Hills Graphics, Kalamazoo, Michigan
Printed in the United States of America

The Directors of Cistercian Publications
in gratitude and appreciation
dedicate this volume to

MISS NANSEMOND LEONARD

TABLE OF CONTENTS

INTRODUCTION

P RAISE. Skip over this word in the titles of these two collections of twelfth-century Marian homilies, and you are off to a bad start. *In PRAISE of the Virgin Mother,* we read; and *On the PRAISES of the Blessed Mary.* Praise, then, is what provides the proper focus for our reading of these texts; praise is what renders the content of these homilies clear and limpid and undistorted.

Meager though the manuscript tradition is for the eight homilies by Amadeus, Bishop of Lausanne, both extant manuscripts agree on the title, *De laudibus beatae Mariae.* And when Bernard of Clairvaux wished to refer to his own cycle of four marian homilies, he explicitly included *praise* in the title: 'I must tell you that I have written . . . four homilies *In Praise of the Virgin Mother,* for that indeed is their proper title,' he writes to the Cardinal Deacon Peter;[1] or again to his friend Oger, a Canon Regular of Mont-Saint-Éloi, 'I am sending you a booklet I wrote not long ago, *In Praise of the Virgin Mother.*'[2]

Those who write learned introductions to works of mediaeval spirituality are surely right when they forewarn the modern-day reader of some of the difficulties which may be encountered: the unfamiliar system of symbols, the use (or apparent abuse) of biblical citations, the flights of rhetoric and the high-blown literary diction which hardly ever come across convincingly in translation. But much more significant and much more characteristic of this kind of devotional literature is the climate of praise that envelops these texts from beginning to end.

Praise seems to be much less a hallmark of contemporary spirituality than was the case in past centuries, and we would do well to keep this in mind as we turn our attention to these twelfth-century homilies in praise of Mary. For the Christian, the spiritual life has always been the fruit of a personal relationship between God and the individual within a community of believers. In an earlier age, people seem to have taken for granted that, in such a relationship, the prime point of reference was God. One's conscious awareness was directed less to the individual's inner experience than to the objective reality of God, and to God's intervention in human history. Self-awareness and great gifts for introspection and psychological analysis there certainly were (Augustine's *Confessions*!); but even where this talent for self-reflection was most developed, the prime point of reference remained, for all that, God. It was all but inevitable that such a keen theocentricism should find expression in a spirituality of praise.

A basic stance of praise is, of course, to be found in all living religions; but this is true in a special sense for the believing Christian: for no other religion teaches that God has entered so absolutely and so definitively into the depths of human existence and experience—the Word was made flesh—and in no other religion has the individual and the community been raised to such heights as sharers in the very life of God—partakers of the divine nature. The response of the believer can hardly be other than a response of praise and thanksgiving.

Scholars are still trying to sort out what happened at the time of the Renaissance. At the risk of overgeneralization, we can at least suggest that, as man became more and more the center of the universe and the measure of that same universe, the emphasis in the relationship between God and man shifted manwards; and as the individual's spiritual experience tended to become increasingly anthropocentric, his capacity to live in a climate of praise waned correspondingly.

Still, the longing to live in a spiritual universe conditioned by an atmosphere of praise remains very much a part of the human experience. No wonder, then, that we find ourselves so deeply moved when, in the grandiose epic of *The Lord of the Rings,* J.R.R. Tolkien describes the triumphant return of the Ring-bearers on the Field of Cormallen, and breaks into the hymn,

> Long live the Halflings! Praise them with great praise!
> Cuio i Pheriain anann' Aglar'ni Pheriannath![3]

We are moved, and deeply moved, because we have within us a desperate longing to hear things praised; and we realize in some obscure way that Tolkien's breaking into Elvish at this point is less a display of his wonted semantic wizardry than a simple admission of the fact that what he is celebrating transcends the possibilities of conventional diction.

The key-note of our two collections of twelfth-century marian homilies is, then, PRAISE. They belong to the genre of praise-literature. And though neither Bernard nor Amadeus breaks into Elvish or indulges himself in the charism of *glossalalia,* their recourse to rhetoric and their use of symbols has something of the same effect. Let us listen to these two men from another age, another civilization, as they praise the high deeds of God, and praise them with great praise.

BERNARD OF CLAIRVAUX AND THE FOUR HOMILIES
IN PRAISE OF THE VIRGIN MOTHER

Saint Bernard's *Homilies in Praise of the Virgin Mother* have a unique place in the writings of the Saint. Almost alone of all his works, these reflections on the gospel-text of the Annunciation were written not for any practical purpose or to answer to a precise pastoral need, but simply to satisfy the exigencies of their author's personal devotion. These homilies are the work of a very young man, and they still give off, for the attentive reader, something of a springtime fragrance and freshness. That this is so is something of a paradox, for there was nothing lightsome or springtime-ish about the circumstances in which they were composed.

Physically frail, chronically ill, and ridiculously young and inexperienced to be, at the age of twenty-five, head of a monastic community, Bernard of Fontaines had been sent from the abbey of Cîteaux in mid-June of 1115, at the head of a group of twelve monks, to found a new abbey in the district of Langres, not far from the river Aube, 'The "Valley of Wormwood" men called it in times past,' writes Bernard's first biographer, William of Saint-Thierry, 'either because of the wormwood growing there in such abundance, or because of the bitter pain experienced by the victims of the local robbers.'[4] In time this Valley of Wormwood was to become the Vale of Light, 'Clairvaux'; but only after a period of much darkness and heartbreak.

By the standards of other mediaeval hagiographical writings, William's portrayal of Bernard's early years as abbot is brutally frank. Saints are sometimes difficult to live with; and Bernard's signal flair for the things of the spirit roused his less gifted companions not only to admiration, but to a perfectly understandable desire to keep a comfortable distance between their unremarkable selves and their quite remarkable abbot. There was not only something more than human in the intensity of Abbot Bernard's spiritual experience, there was something a bit inhuman as well. William's insightful analysis of the relationship between the young Bernard and his community is matched only by his penetrating description of the crisis in Bernard's relations with his monks. From a point of mutual and involuntary estrangement, abbot and community began growing together in the closest possible communion; and Bernard's palpable holiness, which had once seemed to set him apart from and above his brethren, now placed him at the very heart of the community. 'From that time on,' William writes, 'the Holy Spirit began speaking more manifestly in him and through him, giving added impact to his words and deeper insight to his understanding of the Scriptures . . . . '[5] And this was the context in which Bernard composed his homilies in praise of Mary.

The crisis between Bernard and his brethren had left Bernard not only spiritually torn apart, but physically exhausted—so much so that there was danger of imminent death for the young abbot. The diocesan bishop, William of Champeaux, had been following at close hand the struggle of the young community during their heroic days of first beginnings; and it was Bishop William who asked for and obtained from the Cistercian General Chapter a rather remarkable decision: Bernard, Abbot of Clairvaux, was to be under obedience to William of Champeaux, Bishop of Châlons, for the period of a year. William drew up Bernard's rule of life for him, had a special cabin built for him outside the monastery enclosure, and relieved him of all administrative duties.

Bernard's retreat was unpretentious enough: 'the kind of shack people build for lepers next to public cross-roads', writes William of Saint-Thierry.[6] Here in a leper's hut, during the dark hours of the night, the *Homilies in Praise of the Virgin Mother* were born. The regime established for Bernard by William of Champeaux had ruled out for him the long night-vigils practiced by Bernard's brethren in the monastery. But Bernard was allowed to spend at least some part of the night hours in his exercises of devotion. Though freed from the worries of temporal administration, he had to be available to the brethren during the day. This left him brief periods of time in the pre-dawn hours. In darkness, then, and isolated from community-life, the desperately ill young abbot was free for the moment to follow his heart's impulse; and he began singing the high praises of the Virgin Mother and the deep mystery of the Incarnation.

These four homilies were not the first of Bernard's literary production, for they had been preceded a short time before by his *Treatises on the Degrees of Humility and Pride.*[7] They were, however, the first of Bernard's writings devoted to Mary, and they figure at the head of his major marian works—the others being his *Letter 174* to the Canons of Lyon, concerning the conception of Mary;[8] the lengthy sermon 'On the Aqueduct', composed for the feast of the Birth of Mary;[9] and the series of seven Assumption sermons.[10] Secondary marian writings would include some eighteen isolated sermons or sections of sermons and other works.[11]

Our four homilies not only head the list of Bernard's marian writings chronologically, but are, in a sense, the most representative of Bernard's compositions in which Mary features large; for most of the characteristics of the later writings are already to be found here in an especially concentrated form. For the purposes of discussion, the following four characteristics are particularly noteworthy:

1. Bernard's use of Scripture;
2. Bernard as a witness to tradition;
3. Bernard's understanding of Mary's role in the economy of redemption;
4. Bernard's rhetoric in function of praise and theological expression.

1. Mary in the Paradise of Scriptures

Bernard was at his best when ambling through the paradise of Scriptures. There is no doubt, of course, about his ability for systematization and speculative theological thought—we have such writings of his as the treatise *On Grace and Free Choice* or his anti-Abelard disputations to prove the point. Still, neither speculative theology nor theological disputation offered the monk Bernard a milieu in which he could feel comfortably at home. His most congenial habitat was the garden of Holy Writ, in which he could walk and move about freely, listening to God speaking to him in the cool of the evening breeze. Bernard was happiest, then, when he could simply take the word of God, interiorize it, and then communicate it to others with an enthusiasm and a beauty of expression all his own. The homilies *In Praise of the Virgin Mother* are a supreme case in point.

It is characteristic, then, that when Bernard wishes to praise the Virgin Mother, he begins by plunging as deeply as possible into the lukan account of the annunciation. Not a comma escapes his scrutiny. Every word is studied, but studied in a climate of reverence and love. His object is clearly to surrender to the power of God's word through an inner obedience of faith, so as to be drawn by God's word into a personal participation in the life-giving realities made accessible through the sacred text.

Bernard's assimilation of the words of Sacred Scripture is so absolute that his own literary diction is wholly conditioned by it. The Bible has become an organic and living part of his substance, so much so that it becomes virtually impossible for us to reduce Bernard's use of Scripture to any precise system or technique.[12] At times he will study a text with all the objectivity of a modern exegete; biblical words will be used with a maximum of precision, and related texts brought together in such a way that the meaning of each individual text is clarified and re-enforced. At times, a mere allusion, a single contextually significant word or two suffices to provide a biblical dimension or point of reference for what our Abbot is saying. At other times, a text is cited simply as an example. And at still other times, the more serious reader will be alarmed to note that, for all his piety, Bernard, the Last of the Fathers, is weaving into his discourse threads from Holy Writ which have nothing to do, strictly speaking, with what Bernard is saying: mere words or phrases wrenched from the proper context and put to a quite new use. The truth of the matter is that, within Bernard's basic attitude of awe when face to face with the word of God, there is plenty of room for playfulness and for the guileless simplicity and freedom of the sons of God.

Yet another feature of Bernard's biblical thought-patterns and biblical literary diction is this: Bernard encounters the sacred text within a living ecclesial tradition, and assimilates it accordingly. When he cites a biblical text, he cites it, as often as not, according to its shape in the liturgy, or according to the way an Augustine or a Gregory may have quoted it. There is no question, then, of Bernard as a lone individual tête-à-tête with the word of God. His contact with Scripture is always a family affair in which Bernard pores over the sacred page with Origen beside him, and Augustine and Ambrose and Gregory and the anonymous compilers of liturgical texts.

If Bernard wishes to sing the praises of Mary, then, he studies and contemplates her precisely there where God has so perfectly revealed her, in the Scriptures; and, in the company of the Fathers, and with the help of the liturgy, he uses Holy Writ itself to provide both the content of what he wants to say, and the form in which he says it.

2. *Bernard as a Witness to Tradition*

The four homilies *In Praise of the Virgin Mother* are hopelessly unoriginal, at least as regards content. Search though you may, you will be hard pressed to discover a single new idea, a single new interpretation of a biblical text. At the level of content, nothing can be found which cannot be traced to an earlier source—and inevitably a source of unimpeachable orthodoxy.

Bernard's lack of originality and of theological hardihood in Mariology has been variously evaluated. There are some christian thinkers who tend to plot the course of theological investigation as a steady forward-moving progress in which recently acquired insights and funds of knowledge lead on to still further solid acquisitions; and in this way what we know about Mary and her role in salvation history grows more and more explicit as the Church passes through time and history to the final consummation of all things in the world to come. For such theologians it is at the best regrettable, at the worst a bit scandalous, that a Doctor of the Church of Bernard's stature contributed so little in a positive way to the three points of marian teaching which were being developed precisely in Bernard's own twelfth century: the Immaculate Conception of Our Lady, her bodily (and not just spiritual) assumption, and her spiritual maternity. The first Bernard energetically opposed—or more accurately, he opposed the unsatisfactory terms in which the doctrine was being presented at that time; the second he referred to so obliquely that no one knows for sure what his own personal persuasion might have been; and for the third, it was enough for Bernard to be Mary's faithful servant and knight errant, without also being her son. Bernard himself formulated his marian *credo* in unequivocal terms in his famous Letter 174 to the Canons of Lyon, written around 1138–1139[13] to protest the recently introduced celebration of the feast of the Immaculate Conception:

The royal Virgin has in more than abundant measure true titles to honor, true marks of dignity. What need, then, for false claims? Honor her for the integrity of her flesh, the holiness of her life. Marvel at her virginal fecundity, venerate her divine Son. Extol her freedom from concupiscence in conceiving, and from all pain in bringing forth. Proclaim her as reverenced by angels, desired by nations, foretold by patriarchs and prophets, chosen from among all, preferred to all. Magnify her for having found grace, for being mediatrix of salvation and reparatrix of the ages. Exalt her, finally, as one exalted to the heavenly kingdom above the choirs of angels. All this the Church sings to me about her, and teaches me to sing in turn. What I have received from the Church, I firmly hold and confidently pass on to others. Aught else, however, I would scruple to admit . . . [14]

Bernard's theological conservatism extends, however, even to the less profound level of symbol and image; for here, too, he is content to draw on earlier sources. The image of Mary as the aqueduct, spun out at length in the long and lovely Sermon on the Birth of Mary,[15] seems to be Bernard's one claim to originality in the forging of marian imagery.

But what our author lacks in theological adventuresomeness (a lack which some of us will be inclined to applaud), he more than makes up for in intensity and beauty of expression. We note with interest, for example, that Saint Jerome interpreted the name Mary as 'Star of the Sea'; and that this image was given a more ample development in Paschasius Radbertus' ninth-century treatise, *Cogitis me, o Eustochium,* wrongly attributed to Saint Jerome for so many centuries. Our interest is stirred, too, when we are able to track down analagous references to Mary as Star of the Sea in Walfrid Strabo, Fulbert of Chartres, and Peter Damian.[16] But once we have read the closing paragraphs of Bernard's *Homily II,* where the young writer breaks into a hymn in praise of Mary, Star of the Sea, we feel almost as though no one before Saint Bernard had really understood what it means to call upon Mary as 'Star of the Sea'. We can understand, too, why Pope Pius XII chose precisely these lines to quote *in extenso* in the final pages of his encyclical letter on Saint Bernard, *Doctor Mellifluus.*[17]

In brief, Bernard's genius was not that an initiator or innovator, but of a witness to tradition. Without copying, without plagiarizing, he drew ideas and images from traditional sources, and presented them anew with such incomparable beauty that it seemed as though his hearers and readers were discovering them for the first time. For this reason a specialist in Mariology of the stature of the late Fr Henri Barré can spend a substantial number of pages demonstrating convincingly the paucity of Bernard's contribution to the evolution of marian doctrine, and yet conclude by recognizing as wholly justified Bernard's claim to the title 'Marian Doctor' *par excellence.*[18]

3. *Mary's Role in the Economy of Redemption*

So closely has Saint Bernard's name been linked with the full flowering of marian devotion in the twelfth century, that not a few scholars of recent times have felt obliged to correct what seems to them to be a somewhat distorted focus. After all, Bernard's *ex professo* marian writings are quantitatively not all that bulky compared with his sizable literary production as a whole; and we have already seen that Bernard contributed next to nothing to the formulation of a new fund of marian doctrine. Further, few reliable sources contemporary with Bernard refer explicitly to his marian devotion; and even his celebrated childhood vision of the birth of the Infant Jesus is (we are told) something of a hagiographical commonplace. As for the body of marian legends associated with Mary's harper, Bernard, these stories are precisely that: legends without basis in verifiable historical fact.

The more philosophically minded among us are puzzled; because, if all this is true, we are surely face to face with an effect that has no proportionate cause. Perhaps, then, we should look a little closer . . . .

Bernard died at the time of Terce on August 20, 1153—a day within the Octave of the feast of Mary's Assumption into heaven. Geoffrey of

Auxerre, Bernard's personal secretary and intimate, tells us that he was buried a few days later in the abbey church before the altar of Our Lady, 'whose devoted priest he had always been.'[19] But his marian note at the end of Bernard's life corresponds to a marian note towards the beginning of his life, and we might do well to consider briefly the inaugural vision of the child Bernard, hagiographical commonplace though it is supposed to be. As William of Saint-Thierry tells it, with the help of notes supplied by Bernard's faithful amanuensis Geoffrey:

[The boy Bernard] had this vision on the night of the Lord's birth. Everyone was getting ready for the solemn Night Office, as was the custom. For one or another reason, the beginning of the Night Office was somewhat delayed, and Bernard, who was waiting with all the others, seated and with head bowed, dozed off for a few moments. Of a sudden the holy birth of the child Jesus was revealed to the child Bernard, imparting strength and increase to his tender faith, and inaugurating in him the mysteries of divine contemplation. For he (that is to say, the Lord Jesus) appeared as the bridegroom once more coming forth from his chamber. The infant Word, fairer than all the sons of men, appeared before Bernard's eyes as though being born again from the womb of the Virgin Mother, and drawing to himself all the saintly lad's already more than childish love and desire. Bernard was convinced, as he continues to insist to the present day, that this coincided with the exact moment of the Lord's birth. To what extent the Lord showered his blessings on him at that time is clear to those who have heard Bernard preach; for even to this day his understanding of all that touches on this mystery seems to be especially profound, his words especially abounding. Later on he wrote an outstanding work which is among the earliest of his treatises, in praise of the Mother and of her Son, and of his holy birth. The work is based on the gospel text which begins, 'The angel Gabriel was sent by God to a city of Galilee'.[20]

Hagiographical commonplace? Possibly. But what is here important is the fact that so shrewd and insightful an intimate of Bernard as William of Saint-Thierry traces to this Christmas experience of the birth of Christ the beginning of Bernard's life of contemplative prayer. It is through this experience of the Word made flesh that the childhood faith of the boy Bernard begins to mature and develop—and here William's Latin is incomparably beautiful and untranslatable: ' . . . sancta Nativitas, tenerae fidei suggerens incrementa, et divinae in eo inchoans mysteria contemplationis.'[21] Equally to our purpose, however, is the fact that this inaugural vision, which was to bear eventual fruit in the four homilies *In Praise of the Virgin Mother*, brings together Mary and Jesus in the context of the Incarnation. Mary appears, not as

a lone individual, but with her Son, and at the very heart of the
mystery of the Word made flesh. Nor is it by inadvertance that, when
William refers to our four homilies, he extends the official titles and
describes them, not in terms of praise of Mary alone, but as a work 'in
praise of the Mother and of her Son, and of his holy birth'.

There is, then, a wonderful catholic wholeness about Bernard's love
for Mary, which is rooted in his love for Christ. Mother and Son belong
together; and if Bernard has so relatively few works devoted exclusively
to Mary, this is simply because he is constitutionally incapable of isolat-
ing her from her Son or (by extension) from the Church. This explains,
too, why the bulk of 'marian passages' in Bernard's writings are not to
be found in writings devoted specifically or exclusively to Mary, but in
sermons and occasional writings dealing with various aspects of the
Mystery of Christ and the Church.[22] The Fathers of the Second
Vatican Council were of much the same mind as Bernard when, instead
of issuing a separate document on the Blessed Virgin, as originally
planned, they decided instead to include this material as an eighth
chapter in the dogmatic *Constitution on the Church,* under the title,
'The Role of the Blessed Virgin Mary, Mother of God, in the Mystery of
Christ and the Church'.[23]

It would be foolish of us, then, to be deaf to the lyrical accents of an
especially intense love and devotion each time Bernard has occasion to
refer to Mary—a devotion palpable enough to win him the popular title
of *Doctor Marialis;* but it would also be foolish of us not to realize that,
for Bernard, love for Mary was of one piece with love for Christ and
his Church.

4. Bernard's Rhetoric in Function of Praise
   and Theological Expression

Our four homilies are also representative of Bernard's used of
rhetoric in celebration of Christ and of Christ's Mother. To appreciate
the beauty and nobility of Bernard's style,[24] one obviously has to be at
home with Latin, and has to have an ear responsive to music and to
tonal beauty. With Bernard, however, rhetoric is never for the sake of
only the aesthetic response it evokes, but is in function of the com-
munication of truth. Almost always, theological content and literary
form correspond perfectly.

There are admittedly some astute critics who are sharp enough to
detect an unevenness in the excellence of bernardine diction in our four
homilies *In Praise of the Virgin Mother:*[25] there are a few hum-drum

passages, and the writing occasionally smacks of the artificial. These points are well taken (even when voiced by tone-deaf latinists who would probably be hard put to it, had they themselves have to express a thought in a Latin that is both correct and beautiful). As to the occasional levelling off in the quality of our young author's diction, this could well be. It could also well be Bernard's genius for conceiving the part in function of the whole. Take away the speciously more prosaic sections of a Haydn quartet, or liven them up a bit, and the whole musical structure collapses. What is low-keyed prepares for and makes possible the impact of the peak moments of the composition. Haydn was capable, of course, of writing dull music, just as Bernard was capable of turning out a run-of-the-mill sentence. But we should read someone like Bernard of Clairvaux in much the same way that we listen to a Haydn quartet; and quite possibly the occasional 'dull' passages we find would not sound quite so dull if our own capacity for response were less obtuse than it is.

As for the suggestion that Bernard's rhetoric in these homilies is a bit contrived and artificial, one cannot but agree—so long as we take 'artificial' in its proper meaning of 'contrived by art and skill'. Coming as early as they do in Bernard's career as a writer, it would be astonishing indeed if the author were not a bit more self-conscious about literary effect than in his later masterpieces. But the 'artificiality' of these homilies is, in the last analysis, the 'artificiality' of a Bach fugue. Granted, Bernard occasionally over-does it. Take, for instance, the Latin text of the passage from *Homily III,* where our author asks the question, 'What sort of son' is Mary's child to be? The answer comes in the form of a poem, as can easily be seen if we respect the inner structure of the passage:

> Illius eris mater,
> cuius Deus est pater.
> Filius paternae claritatis
> erit corona tuae caritatis.
> Sapientia paterni cordis
> erit fructus uteri virginalis.
> > Deum denique paries,
> > et de Deo concipies.
> Confortare ergo, Virgo fecunda,
> casta puerpera, mater intacta . . . . [26]

The Latin text ripples along, then, in five sets of verses with a corresponding rhyme-scheme; a-a, b-b, c-c, d-d, e-e; and even the syllable-count forms a pattern: 7-7, 10-11, 10-11, 8-8, 11-11. Fr Anselme Dimier, who was the first to draw attention to this particular example of Bernard the poet, remarked that it would be nice to hear the text set to music.[27] But why? It is already music enough as it is.

§

Whatever imperfections our four homilies might betray by reason of their young author's inexperience, generations of appreciative readers have been unmindful of any serious difficulty. The texts were copied and recopied, and soon ranked high in the list of the Mellifluous Doctor's most widely circulated and most popular works. Even at the present time two substantial passages have been included in the Liturgy of the Hours: *Homily IV,* 8–9 (Office of Readings for December 20) and *Homily II,* 1-2, 4 (Office of Readings for Tuesday of the Twentieth Week in Ordinary Time).

As is the case with so many other writings of the Saint, Fr Jean Leclercq, in preparing his critical edition of the Latin text, was easily able to identify three distinct forms of the text: 1. a brief recension corresponding to the earliest redaction; 2. a somewhat longer version represented chiefly by manuscripts connected with germanic monasteries belonging to the filiation of Morimond, the fourth daughter-house of Cîteaux; 3. and, finally, the 'perfect' or final recension, which is the last of a series of editorial ameliorations carried out either by Bernard himself or under his personal aegis.[28]

AMADEUS OF LAUSANNE AND HIS EIGHT HOMILIES
ON THE PRAISES OF THE BLESSED MARY

The last of Amadeus of Lausanne's eight homilies begins with a gentle complaint: 'Several days, beloved, have passed in which, under the burden of the episcopate and encumbered with great anxieties, I have been unable to provide your holy hunger the promised meal concerning the praise of blessed Mary.' Any conscientious bishop could, of course, refer in all honesty to the burden of his office and to his great anxieties. But Bishop Amadeus had better reasons to do so than have most. Amadeus had become bishop at a particularly tense period in the history of the vast diocese of Lausanne. Political difficulties and the irregularity of his personal life had forced the resignation of Amadeus' immediate predecessor, Guy de Maligny;[29] and Bishop Guy's fourteen years as Bishop of Lausanne, 1130–1144, and only served to exacerbate the chronic tensions between ecclesiastical authority and the wielders of secular power. Like Bishop Guy, Amadeus was to have an episcopacy of fourteen years, from 21 January 1145 (date of his consecration—he was elected earlier, in 1144) until his holy death on 27 August 1159. Unlike Bishop Guy, however, Amadeus brought to his high office all the qualifications of a saintly pastor of souls and of a capable administrator —qualifications which were to be tested to the utmost. As late as 1156 or thereabouts, Amadeus was forced to write his Easter Pastoral Letter[30] from a place of exile. The long-term open war being waged against him by his homonymn, Amadeus de Genevois, had reached a particularly acute stage; and it was more than a bit ironic that the official charge of the rebel Amadeus was that of *advocatus* or *avoué* of the Church of Lausanne, the official whose responsibility it was to protect the temporal interests of his bishop.

Our homilies should be read against this background of violence and civil unrest simply because this was the *Sitz im Leben* in which they were composed, and because this somber real-life background brings out all the more the startlingly bright colors and radiant lights given off by these eight homilies. Page after page abounds in the luxuriant imagery of flowers, precious stones and gleaming jewels, gentle incense-laden breezes and fragrance of rare spices. True, the imagery becomes, at times, over-sumptious; our senses become glutted. But even so, we ought to appreciate the springtime verdure because it contrasts so strikingly with the winter bleakness of Amadeus' usual landscape.

This is not to suggest that the concrete situation in which Amadeus carried out his difficult episcopal duties represents reality, and that the spiritual world depicted in such vibrant colors in the homilies represents an unreal world. Both worlds are real; or—better—both worlds form a single whole. But it remains true to say that the world of faith, so immediately present to the vision of the Bishop of Lausanne, relativizes the all-importance most of us attach to the passing moment of our historically conditioned personal situation. Like each of us, Amadeus can experience to the full the impact of a given moment. There is nothing 'supra-temporal', for instance, in a letter he wrote from exile, in which he depicts an especially grisly scene: he has just finished celebrating Mass, and one of his followers is murdered even as Amadeus clasps him in a protective embrace; the episcopal vestments run red with the victim's blood.[31] But for all the immediacy of the present moment, Amadeus habitually remains conscious above all of the whole broad sweep of sacred history extending from the creation of all things to the final consummation of all things in the world to come; and it is this panoramic, totalizing vision which is responsible for the remarkable unity of the eight homilies *On the Praises of the Blessed Mary*. But before we look a bit closer at these twelfth-century texts, a further word should be said about their rather impressive author.

The Curriculum Vitae *of Amadeus of Lausanne*

'God in whom we hope is present,' writes Amadeus in *Homily III*; and he adds one of the extremely rare autobiographical remarks to be found in these homilies: 'in him we have from our youth up been taught to trust' (p. 79).

Amadeus' religious formation began, in fact, well before the days of his youth. He was only a few years past the days of his babyhood when his father, Lord Amadeus d'Hauterives, of the ancient and noble house of Clermont, turned apostle of monastic life and, sometime around 1119, brought to the newly founded Cistercian Abbey of Bonnevaux, near Vienne, not only himself but his ten-year old boy, Amadeus Junior, but seventeen knight-companions as well.[32] Whatever else the senior Amadeus had given up in coming to the poor, struggling community of Bonnevaux, he had not given up the idea that his son should receive a solid education. At Bonnevaux the lad did begin receiving an education, but hardly of the sort deemed suitable by his concerned father. The philosophy of education held by the saintly Abbot John, the biographer somewhat sententiously tells us, was that 'the anointing of the Paraclete could teach the lad more in a second than the teachings of an apostate grammarian like Priscian in a stretch of many years'.[33] The force of the argument was lost on Amadeus Senior. In a moment of depression he apostasized; and one day, probably in the year 1122, he took his son and rode off with him to the great abbey of Cluny, with its tradition of enlightened humanism. The account of Amadeus Senior's brief, unhappy life as a monk of Cluny, his anguished repentance, and his return to Bonnevaux, belongs to another story. But if Bonnevaux could not provide Amadeus Junior with a suitable education, neither could Cluny; for almost immediately the lad was sent for further studies to the court of his kinsman, Conrad of Hohenstaufen, the future Emperor Conrad III. The three years Amadeus spent in Germany could hardly have sufficed to complete the education of the adolescent, but we nevertheless find him in 1125, shortly after having fulfilled the minimum age-requirement for accep-tance as a Cistercian novice, knocking at the gate of Clairvaux. Clairvaux, of course, was the preferred monastic retreat for young aristocrats and university drop-outs.

At Clairvaux, the education begun spasmodically and continued at the court of Conrad reached its term. For fourteen years young Amadeus had the joy of living under the tutelage of Saint Bernard him-self; and it was in this setting of Clairvaux, with all its contagious enthu-siasm, *devotio iocunda,* and seriousness of purpose, that the stripling Amadeus grew to full manhood. The attainments of the mature Ama-deus must have impressed even Saint Bernard, who, in 1139, deemed him ready to become abbot of the Savoyard abbey of Hautecombe. This monastery had been founded much earlier in the century, but had become affiliated with the Cistercian Order only in 1135. Amadeus' abbacy coincided with the change of location of the original abbey and the construction of the monastic buildings; and it was also under Amadeus that the consolidation of the Cistercian ideals in the recently affiliated community took place.

The young abbot's gifts as administrator and spiritual father were considerable enough to draw attention to him well outside the imme-diate sphere of the Cistercian family. For when the deplorable Guy de Maligny finally resigned his episcopal dignity in 1144, it was the thirty-four year old Abbot Amadeus of Hautecombe whom the clergy and faithful of Lausanne chose to succeed Bishop Guy. Accepting the burden of the episcopal office only at the insistence of Pope Lucius II, Bishop Amadeus remained very much Amadeus the monk. At no time during the troubled fourteen years of his episcopacy did the faithful of Lausanne find reason to regret their choice of pastor; and when Ama-deus died on 27 August 1159, those who were with him were well aware that they were assisting at the death-bed of a saint. The liturgical memorial of Saint Amadeus of Lausanne is celebrated to this day, and is assigned in the Cistercian calendar of saints to August 30.[34]

The Homilies

The literary remains of Amadeus of Lausanne are all but coterminous with the eight homilies *On the Praises of the Blessed Mary.* Apart from these, only two letters survive: the first to Count Humbert of Savoy (around 1148);[35] the second, the pastoral letter already mentioned earlier, and addressed to the faithful of the diocese during the painful months of the bishop's enforced exile in or around 1156.[36] Also extant from the years of Amadeus' episcopacy are some fourteen official acts or fragments of acts;[37] and there is an outside chance that a page-long set of pastoral directives for confessors should be added to the list of Amadeus' writings.[38] But clearly, Amadeus' only serious claim to consideration as an author is his series of eight homilies devoted to the praises of Our Lady.

True, these homilies contain several allusions to their actually having been preached as a series of popular sermons in honor of the Mother of God—see, for instance, the *exordium* to *Homily VIII.* But medievalists are there to caution us about taking such references too seriously. They are, we are often and rightly told, a literary device to be found in more than one sermon destined not to be preached aloud in church, but to be pondered over by the devout reader in the privacy of his room or cloister cranny. It would, of course, be unrealistic to envisage Amadeus declaiming these rather elegant Latin texts before a cathedral congregation of people ignorant of Latin. But there is no need to propose the counter-hypothesis that the congregation was composed not of the people at large, but of the lettered cathedral clergy. After all, the polished Latin text we have before us, if we care to look at the edition in the Abbé Migne's *Patrologia Latina,* Tome 188,[39] or—still better—the the fine edition of the Latin text established by Dom Jean Deshusses (a Benedictine monk of the very abbey where Amadeus was once abbot) in *Sources chrétiennes* 72,[40] represents only one particular form of the text. We would hardly be wrong to presume a whole evolution in the history of the text as it passed through various stages from Amadeus' first rough notes scratched on wax-tablets to the final redaction in phrases of an elegant, sonorous (but somewhat limited) latinity. The existence of a Latin text in no way excludes the possibility or even near certainty that these sermons were indeed delivered by Amadeus before an appreciative audience—but in the living language of his hearers, and in a version related to, but not necessarily identical with the polished Latin text.

The printed history of these homilies is out of all proportion to the paucity of the manuscript evidence. Manuscript L 303 of the Canton Library of Fribourg (Switzerland) dates from the thirteenth century, and comes from the nearby Cistercian abbey of Hauterive.[41] There is a second manuscript (without classification-number) from the Cathedral Chapter Library of Aosta, Italy; but this dates only from the fifteenth century.[42] Unimportant are the folios with a bit more than two of the homilies in the fifteenth-century Lausanne breviary manuscript, L 125 of the Canton Library, Fribourg.[43] The printed editions begin with the *editio princeps* printed at Basel in 1517, and prepared by the erudite Gervasus Sopherus. The text he followed was independent of the recoverable extant manuscripts; but since our humanist editor took the liberty of touching up Amadeus' Latin as often as it proved offensive to his delicate classical ear, this edition has to be used with caution; and since it was this edition which served as the basis of all subsequent editions, the same caution has to be repeated in every instance.[44] In practice, we would do well to ignore all the numerous editions prior to the *Sources chrétiennes* edition of 1960.[45]

Is Amadeus a good writer? Absolutely, so long as we refrain from comparing him with an absolute master such as Saint Bernard. Amadeus' sentences flow along in balanced periods; and he is particularly careful about the rhythm of the cadences. This makes for a pleasing musicality. Much less pleasing because of its cumulative effect is Amadeus' compulsive recourse to series based on the mystic number three. It is not enough for Amadeus to write at the beginning of *Homily I* that 'this blessed Virgin [is] more brilliant than every light'; he instinctively re-enforces the statement by adding that she is 'more pleasing than every sweetness, more eminent than every dominion'. So long as this happens at the rate of no more than two or three times a page, the effect is not displeasing. When it happens more often, the reader begins to feel uncomfortable. But let the impatient reader take note! The theological content of the passage is usually rich in direct proportion to the multiplication of ternary groups. Thus, when Amadeus rings the changes on the Philippians hymn (Ph 2:9-10) in *Homily VI,* he is simply spinning out the Pauline series: 'things in heaven, things on earth, things under the earth.' 'In truth,' writes Amadeus,

1. the knee of those in HELL   bends before him in DREAD,
   the knee of those on EARTH   through SELF-INTEREST
   of those in HEAVEN   through their BLESSEDNESS.

2. On the FIRST   he INFLICTS PUNISHMENT,
   the SECOND   he BRINGS OUT FROM THEIR WRETCHEDNESS,
   the THIRD   he RAISES IN GLORY.

3. To the FIRST he is TERRIBLE   in JUDGEMENT,
   to the SECOND   PITYING   in AIDING them,
   to the THIRD   GENEROUS   in REWARDING them.

4. He SUBDUES   the DEMONS   with his SWORD,
   REDEEMING   MEN   with his BLOOD,
   SATISFYING   the ANGELS with the SIGHT OF HIS COUNTENANCE.

5. Therefore HELL bends the knee, TREMBLING at his POWER;
   EARTH bows the knee,   PRAISING   his MERCY.
   HEAVEN bends the knee,   CRYING OUT: 'Holy, holy . . . '

The final member comes as a shock because the pattern is broken.
Clearly, Amadeus should have written: 'Heaven bends the knee, crying
out at his GLORY: "Holy, holy . . . ".' A few lines later, Amadeus
brings Mary into the pattern established by the Pauline text, and shows
how Christ has made her a sharer in his own lordship over heaven, earth,
and hell:

1. 'He has brought to you
      the SOVEREIGNTY OF HEAVEN   through his GLORY,
      the KINGDOM OF THE WORLD   through his MERCY,
      the SUBJECTION OF HELL   through his POWER.

2. All things with their diverse feelings respond to your great and
   unspeakable glory:
      ANGELS   by HONOR,
      MEN   by LOVE,
      DEMONS by TERROR.

3. For you are
      VENERATED in HEAVEN,
      LOVED   in the WORLD,
      FEARED   in HELL.'

Amadeus' thought seems to move in triplets. We might wish at times that he had been a bit more subtle, that he had given free reign less often to his obsession with ternary patterns. But we also have to admit that as often as not this ternary grouping corresponds to. three objective stages or levels of reality, and that the literary threesomes correspond to a tripartite theological reality, or at least to a theological reality which admits to a tripartite analysis.

Apart from his concern for the rhythmic *cursus* of his cadences, and his ternary phrases. Amadeus' recourse to the tricks of the rhetorical trade are minimal. An occasional rhyme or assonance is probably simply fortuitous; and there is next to none of the wordplay so characteristic of writers such as Bernard. When we read in the Latin text of *Homily III,* for instance, that the incarnate Word 'implevit *sacratissimum* et *secretissimum sacra*mentum', we have before us an exception which proves the rule; so also in the phrase from *Homily VII:* 'Ibi *orienti* magis quam *morienti, et abiturae* plus quam *obiturae . . . .* ' Whatever other difficulties of translation these homilies afford, Amadeus has signally lightened the translator's task by avoiding the systematic use of assonance, consonance, rhyme, alliteration, and other forms of word-jugglery.

At the same time, Amadeus makes considerable demands on the reader, as do most of the really fine twelfth-century Cistercian spiritual writers. They take for granted that the reader will be actively participating in the work at hand. The author has 'created' the text, so to speak; but it is up to the reader to accomplish the work of 'co-creation'. Amadeus gives us the image of a lily. He expects us to make that image our own; to be able to visualize what a lily looks like; to experience what its particular quiet splendor among flowers really is. He assumes that we know how to breathe in the fragrance of that lily, that we know how to admire its beauty. The problem with Amadeus, however, is that he keeps our spiritual senses and imaginative faculties working overtime. His pages teem with such a profusion of sights and sounds and fragrances and textures and tastes that there is danger of our becoming glutted by the superabundance of the fare—at least if we take seriously the work of 'co-creating' the text we are reading.

We moderns, truth to tell, are at rather a disadvantage compared with the reader of an earlier age. We are used to the realistic novel, to *verismo* opera, to the brutal explicitness of TV and the cinema. Everything is spelled out; our imagination is insulted; the work of conjuring up the images is done for us; and our interior senses are assaulted by the very violence of the medium to which we are exposed. In the case of mediaeval literature of the sort represented by these homilies, however, our role has got to be more active, more creative. We must learn, too, how to approach these texts in a frankly sensual manner; and our ability to do so is hard won these days. Most of us simply do not have the interior freedom requisite to make use of our senses in a fully human way; and this sort of freedom can be had only at the cost of a radical asceticism.

There is a difficulty on yet another score. The language of Amadeus is a symbolic language composed chiefly of biblical imagery (though more than one classical allusion or choice of words attests to Amadeus' exposure to the Latin classics). It is easier, certainly, to track down Amadeus' scriptural citations and allusions than is the case of Bernard of Clairvaux, since Amadeus is a bit more bald and explicit in the way he uses his borrowed language. Still, the basic difficulty caused by our relative unfamiliarity with the point of reference assumed by Amadeus remains. There is no question but that the biblical citations and allusions woven into our author's discourse contain clear ideas, precise concepts; but they also open out into other related directions. For all their precision, these biblical images and biblical statements function less as definitions setting precise limits to reality than as doors opening into deeper levels of understanding and experience.

We need not be too concerned over the fact, then, that we could be missing something by our inability to follow through with the rich implications of Amadeus' symbolic language. Missing something we certainly are; but what remains will be rich enough, for all that. Neither would Amadeus take it amiss if we occasionally read something into the text which he did not intend. This can be to our advantage, so long as what we read into the text harmonizes with the basic meaning of that text. Though the distinction would probably be lost on our author, he practises not only *exegesis* (reading *out of* the text) but *eisegesis* (reading *into* the text); and there is no reason why his readers should not do likewise. Amadeus was not interested in a text as an objective phenomenon existing in itself and independent of its readers or hearers. His concern was that the objective text be interiorized and rendered fruitful by those who make that text their own. Great care, then, should be taken at the level of explicit ideas and clear conceptual formulations; but to strip away the imagery and allusions and expressive overtones would be like analyzing the harmonic progressions of Bach's d minor *Chaconne,* and substituting this for the actual experience of playing or hearing the d minor *Chaconne.*

No one, absolutely no one, is going to catch all the allusions or spin out all the implications of Amadeus' language; and not many readers will be in a position to catch the monastic resonance and liturgical dimensions of Amadeus' citations. Take, for instance, the *exordium* to *Homily II,* in which Amadeus exhorts us to hasten through the vivid brightness of Mary's paths 'with swelling heart and unspeakable joy' (p. 69). Do we recognize here a discreet allusion to the final lines of the Prologue to the *Holy Rule,* where Saint Benedict assures the tyro that, 'As we progress in our monastic life and in faith, *our hearts will be en-larged,* and *we shall run* with *unspeakable sweetness* of love in the way of God's commandments'. A quick check of the respective Latin texts confirms the parallels: ' . . . dilatato corde et inenarrabili percurramus laetitia' (Amadeus); 'dilatato corde, inenerrabili dilectionis dulcedine curritur' (Benedict). Moreover, the context of the two texts is rather similar: Mary grows in love as she pursues the path marked out for her in salvation history; while the monk grows in love as he pursues the path marked out for him by God's commandments. If we now begin pondering the parallelism between the dynamic thrust of Mary's *curriculum vitae* and the dynamic thrust of the program for monks traced out by Saint Benedict in his *Holy Rule,* we shall probably be indulging in *eisegesis* rather than *exegesis;* but this is not to suggest that such *eisegesis* would be unprofitable for the reader. Relatively few readers could have been expected to catch on their own any parallel between the above quoted line of *Homily II* and the Prologue to the *Holy Rule.* Such readers will have missed out on an interesting thought worth their exploring in greater detail. But they have not missed out on everything, for they will still be able to grasp perfectly well the essential point Amadeus is making: Mary's life meant a constant growth in love.

Or again, take the mini-citation of Hebrews 7:4 in *Homily I* (p. 65) —six whole words: 'Behold how great is he.' The reader who enjoys verifying biblical quotations such as this one is bound to be a bit non-plussed upon finding that the author of Hebrews is here referring, not directly to Christ, but to his Old Testament prefigurement, Melchizedek. Is Amadeus handling his Scripture quotation with too light a hand? In point of fact, Amadeus is not quoting Scripture at all— at least, not directly. He is quoting a Night Office responsory: 'Behold, how great is he who comes forth to save the nations—Intuemini quantus sit qui ingreditur ad salvandas gentes.' This responsory was once in general use in the Latin West in the Night Office for the Fourth Sunday of Advent. For Amadeus and his readers, the text would have carried with it a strong resonance of the final days of Advent when the birth of Christ, made present through the celebration of the liturgy, is almost upon us. The perceptive Cistercian monk or nun would also recall that this same responsory did additional service in the Cistercian Night Office for the Feast of the Annunciation, 25 March. It is helpful

to be aware of these resonances when we read the text of Amadeus'
homily—helpful, but not per-essential; for what Amadeus has written
makes glorious sense even if we fail to hear the expressive overtones,
even if we do not feel ourselves bathed in the climate created by the
liturgy of late Advent.

Amadeus' use of biblical texts can be particularly disconcerting with
respect to his disturbing penchant for applying to Mary texts which
are immediately applicable only to Christ. 'As death entered the world
through a *woman,* so through a *woman* did life enter', we read in
Homily II (p. 74), where our author adapts Romans 5:12 to suit his
marian context, and then straightway proceeds to do the same with
1 Corinthians 15:22: 'And as in *Eve* all died, so in *Mary* all rose again'
(ibid.). We recognize, of course, the patristic theme of Mary as the New
Eve, even while we regret that Amadeus touched on this classical
parallel only by giving to the biblical texts a twist some of us might
deem uncalled for. We are, after all, sensitive to the justifiable
criticism of those theologians who rightly take exception to the kind of
marian devotion which tends in any way to isolate Mother from Son.
In this instance, Amadeus seems to be going a step farther by substituting the Mother for the Son.

The objection is a bit specious; and, if anything, Amadeus'
tendency lies in the direction clean contrary to the objection that he
disassociates Mother from Son. Central to our author's approach is the
implicit conviction that christian existence means life in Christ, means
sharing in Christ and his mysteries. Quite simply, Mary is the one who,
in God's plan of salvation history, stands closest to Christ; she is the
one who shares most perfectly in all the particular mysteries which
make up the total Mystery of Christ. The stages of Mary's growth as
treated of by Amadeus are so many stages in her participation in the
Mystery of Christ. The Pauline formula of life *in* Christ and life *with*
Christ is predicable of any Christian who measures up to the exigencies
of his vocation; but it is predicable of Mary to a supreme degree. Moreover, Mary's closeness to her Son means closeness to what Saint
Augustine styled the 'Whole Christ', that is to say, Head and members,
Christ and his Church. Here, however, the point is that the identifica-
tion of Mary with Christ and the things of Christ is so absolute that,
much to our discomfort, Amadeus can apply to Mary biblical texts
which apply directly only to the Lord Jesus. Usually he is careful to add
a saving qualifying expression. When he tells us in *Homily VII* (p. 120),
for instance, that the fulness of divinity remained in Mary bodily
(a re-phrasing of Col 2:9) he is careful to add: *mediante Christo*—the
fulness of divinity is within Mary bodily, because Christ, the incarnate

Word, is within Mary bodily in the months preceding his birth at Bethlehem.

Perhaps Amadeus' understanding of the relationship between Mary and her Son, between Mary and the Church, can best be seen by a quick glance at the general thematic outline of our eight homilies:

MARY IN SALVATION HISTORY

Homily I	General Introduction: Mary between Two Testaments
Homily II	Introductory Schema of the stages of participation in salvation history, each stage of which forms the theme of one of the homilies to follow.
	Stage One (Homily II in strict sense) Justification of Mary; her embellishment with all the virtues in view of her unique vocation.
Homily III	*Stage Two:* Mary's nuptial union with the Holy Spirit; the virginal conception of Christ.
Homily IV	*Stage Three:* Mother of the Saviour; the virgin birth.
Homily V	*Stage Four:* The sword through Mary's heart; Mary and the redemption wrought by Christ.
Homily VI	*Stage Five:* The joy of Mary; Christ's Resurrection, Ascension, Glorification.
Homily VII	*Stage Six:* Mary's assumption into heaven; image of the future glory of the Church in heaven.
Homily VIII	*Stage Seven:* Final consummation or perfection; all Israel is saved.

The panorama is a vast one. Indeed, considering the fact that it begins with creation and the fall, and ends only with the final consummation of mankind in the world to come, it could hardly be more vast or more all-comprehending. Important for the matter at hand, then, is the fact that Amadeus views the Mother of God not only in the closest possible proximity to Christ and his Church, but views her against the whole sweep of salvation history. Further, all her titles to glory, all her prerogatives are displayed for us only in the context of Mary's place and role in the unfolding of the Mystery of Christ.

Amadeus' approach is essentially that of a theologian rather than that of an exegete—though we should feel a bit uncomfortable about pushing the distinction too far! Still, while the exegete begins with a biblical text and sees what ought to be drawn from it, the theologian tends to begin with the faith of the Church which he tries to understand and clarify by recourse to the inspired word and texts from tradition. The structure of Saint Bernard's homilies *In Praise of the*

apples, for I am sick with love' (Sg 2:5). These blossoms or flowers are nothing other than the Old Testament adumbrations to individual mysteries which make up the total Mystery of Christ; and the 'apples' are the actual realization of all that had been foretold. This provides Amadeus with the elaborate picture he now paints, in which Mary is portrayed standing between two golden baskets filled with fruits and decked with flowers—the Old Testament and the New. And if the reader objects that he would prefer to see Mary, not between two baskets, but with her Child in her arms, that reader has missed the point. Mary is here placed at the meeting point between the two Testaments. She is at the very center where shadow becomes reality; and it is not enough for her simply to hold her Child in a mother's embrace: the fruit stands for the working out of all that makes up the total Mystery of Christ. So now Amadeus begins spelling out in detail the various stages in the unfolding of the panoramic plan for mankind's salvation—a plan in which Mary is beside her Son at every stage of its unfolding. The reader would be well-advised to go slowly at this point. Symbol is heaped upon symbol in luxuriant profusion, and the rapid scanning of a paragraph can result only in confusion for an impatient reader. The essential thread of Amadeus' argument is that the two Testaments are in accord. This he demonstrates by showing how: 1. the Old Testament *foretells* Christ and his Mother, and 2. the New Testament *reveals* Christ and his Mother. There is a final excursus in which Amadeus interprets the Holy of Holies and its furnishings in terms of Christological (and marian) typology.

Homily II continues the preceding by adding to the portrait of Mary a detailed depiction of her splendid apparel and ornaments—images of the gifts and graces bestowed on her by reason of her high destiny as Mother of the incarnate Word. But Amadeus first states the general theme that Mary's life meant an uninterrupted progress and growth in love and virtue; and it is the stages in this spiritual journey which form the subject-matter of the homilies to follow. Amadeus summarizes the themes (already outlined earlier, p. xxxiii), and then relates each stage of Mary's progress with one of the gifts of the Holy Spirit. We can only be thankful that he contents himself with this, and stops short of relating the seven stages of Mary's progress to the seven petitions of the Lord's Prayer . . . . We now reach what, for the modern reader, is probably the most difficult part of the entire cycle of homilies: a detailed allegorical interpretation of everything that makes for Mary's beauty. Her apparel is analyzed on the score of its dazzling whiteness, its fragrance, its precious costliness, its variety (different colors, different purposes for each article of clothing). This is followed by a parallel allegorical interpretation of the various parts of Mary's body; after which Amadeus returns once again to each item of clothing in Mary's wardrobe. This homily is a gold mine for the specialist in mediaeval fashion-plates, but for most of us the text will be a bit difficult. Perhaps it might help to recall the tendency in times past to turn articles of clothing into allegories. Saint Paul did it with his bucklers and helmets and breastplates and shoes and the like; and until very recent times, the priest vested for Mass while praying brief formulas based on an allegorical interpretation of each article he was putting on. What marks Amadeus off as exceptional here is simply the ampleness and ruthless thoroughness of his allegorical analysis. But let us be careful not to lose sight of the spiritual realities which are, after all, the real object of our author's discourse.

Homily III deals with the Incarnation and the virginal conception of our Lord. It begins with a moving prayer addressed to God the Father, whose love is so overwhelming that even omnipotent God cannot keep it within limits. All that follows, then, is a celebration of God's love.

The homily belongs to the type structured on a consideration of the *circumstances* surrounding the subject under discussion: who? why? how? for what purpose? Amadeus focusses his attention directly on the incarnate Word, and asks: 'Where have you come from?' The answer is: from the Trinity, from all three Persons. After a moving confession of man's impotence at discoursing on such deep realities, our theologian— and here Amadeus is obviously enjoying himself—explains briefly in what sense Christ comes not only from the Father and from the Holy Spirit, but from the Word. Next a splendid development based on the classical figures of the Incarnation: the rock, the fleece, the earth—all of which is a preparation for his presentation of the actual realization of the mystery heralded by the Old Testament types. The Virgin conceives the incarnate Word through the action of the Holy Spirit; and Amadeus reflects in glowing terms on the fulness of Mary's grace and on the action of both Holy Spirit and of Word within her. The homily ends in the best mediaeval tradition with an apostrophe addressed to Mary, in which Amadeus asks her what it must have been like to become Mother of the Word made flesh.

Homily IV, on the birth of Christ, is one of the longest of the eight homilies, and the least systematic as regards structure. The reader whose ear is attuned to classical literature will be startled and delighted to find Amadeus, in his *exordium,* describing the union of natures in Christ in terms borrowed from the legend of Orpheus and his lyre. Jesus is the new Orpheus; and it is to the music given off by the Sacred Humanity that we begin contemplating the virginal birth of the

Lord. It was as virgin that Mary had conceived him, and it is as virgin that she now brings him forth. Mary is the New Eve; and Christ is the 'hand of God' (another favorite patristic image) which has brought life and healing and deliverance to countless numbers. Christ's birth, then, could only mean a perfecting, a consummating of Mary's virginity. The mystery is, of course, too much for us; and Amadeus, in a passage which deserves inclusion in any anthology of texts on faith and reason, asks us how we can expect to sound the depths of the mysteries of God when we cannot even fathom the mystery of a tiny mosquito. He insists, though, that 'he who does not know himself does not penetrate the deep things of God'. This entire passage is directed, it would seem, to Christians who exalt unreasonably the autonomy of reason (are there here overtones of the polemic crystallized in the affair of Master Peter Abelard?). But now Amadeus apostophizes two other categories of non-believers. There is an exhortation to the Jews not to refuse what Amadeus sees as the fulfillment of the Old Testament prophecies precisely through the virginal birth of the Messiah. This type of address is frequent in mediaeval literature. Much less frequent, however, is the last of these three exhortations, which is addressed to 'gentiles', that is to say, to Mohammedans; and it would seem that Amadeus is here borrowing freely from Peter the Venerable's tract *Adversus nefandam sectam Saracenorum.*[50] Just as Amadeus began his treatment of the virginal birth by referring to the Eve–Mary parallel, so also he returns to the same parallel to close this section of the homily. He is now beyond polemics, and he breaks into a hymn about the joy of the universe at the birth of Christ; and when he begins speaking about the mysteriousness of the night of the Saviour's birth, his Latin rises to heights of incomparable beauty. There is nothing finer even in Saint Bernard's Christmas sermons. Saint Francis at Greccio is anticipated in the warm tenderness of Amadeus' meditation on Mary's joy at the birth of her Son in whom the hopes and aspirations of all ages now meet. But there is no *Schwärmerei* in any of this, and the intensity of the human dimension is achieved precisely because the divine is ever present.

The Wisdom of the Father clung round her neck and in her arms rested the Power that moves all things. The little Jesus stood on his mother's lap and in her virgin bosom rested that rest of holy souls. Sometimes tilting his head while she held him with right hand or left, he bent his gentle gaze upon his mother, he whom angels longed to look upon, and called her mother with sweet murmur, he whom every spirit calls in time of need.[51]

With *Homily V* we are plunged into the Passion of the Lord. Amadeus begins with a distinction between two types of martyrdom:

that of the body, that of the soul. The Old Testament offers a number
of martyrs of the heart: Abraham with knife in hand to slay his only
son; Moses more than ready to die if only his people can be spared;
David praying that the angel's sword turned towards his people be
turned rather against himself. But the martyrdom of Mary at the foot
of the cross surpasses all possibility of human reckoning.

*She stood near the cross that she might see her son's sweet head
anointed with oil above his fellows', beaten with rods and crowned with
thorns—heart-rending sight! She saw there was neither form nor beauty
in him who was lovely with a beauty beyond the sons of men. She
saw him who was high above all nations despised and of no reputation,
the holy of holies crucified with criminals and malefactors, the eyes of
the lofty man brought low, the head of the sustainer of all things sagging
to his shoulders, the radiant face of God wither away and the glory
of his countenance hidden.*[52]

This God, then, is a hidden God; and Amadeus the theologian now
sums up briefly traditional patristic teaching (Augustine, Leo, Gregory)
on the weakness of God as the means of the defeat of Satan. This leads
to the long lament over the Chosen People who remain unmoved before
God crucified, even as the universe takes part in the cosmic demonstra-
tion of bitter grief. The rhetoric begins like that of the standard
mediaeval passages and tracts *Contra Iudaeos,* but it ends on a quite
different note: love. Mary's martyrdom is caused not only by reason of
her love for Jesus, but also by reason of her love for her own people.
The final word, the inalterable word, is love, not hate. The final pages
of this deeply moving threnody on the death of Jesus are devoted to
the compassion of Mary, to the *Mater dolorosa,* and to the example of
Mary's constancy and courage.

With *Homily VI* we find ourselves at the paschal banquet over
which Mary presides. This is a wedding banquet, and the bread is the
bread of life; the wine, the wine of the resurrection. Milk, honey, fatted
calf—images of light, holy mirth, and universal joy succeed in rapid
succession as Amadeus attempts to capture the note of paschal joy. If
the faithful at large experience joy at the victory of Christ, what is the
joy experienced by his Mother? So closely identified with Jesus is
Mary that his victory is her victory. At this point, however, the paschal
experience concentrated in a special way in Christ the Victor and his
Mother begins reaching out to embrace a new human race. Christ was
the seed that fell into the earth and died that it might bear much fruit.
'He laid himself down at seed time that he might at the harvest gather
the human race' (p. 111). The images become gloriously confused, and
the earth in which this divine seed took root becomes Mary's womb,

but also the baptismal font of the Church. A startling allusion to a single word from the Song of Songs—*acervus,* 'heap'—begins a long development based on images from that same Song. Mary's womb is the womb from which Christ is born, and it is also the womb from which the Mystical Body of Christ is born. The lilies of the Song of Songs are so many words of Scripture in affirmation of the Bride's virginal purity and beauty; and somehow Mary and Church become fused. The breasts of the Bride-Church are the two Testaments, providing nourishment suited to the condition of each of the children of the Church. The lilies return in yet another passage, but this time they are the souls of the saints who surround Mary, and who owe their beauty and their flowering to the victory won by Christ. The image of flowering reminds us, at least implicitly, that all flesh is grass, doomed to wither away. So Amadeus develops the theme that Christ flowers, not like the grass but as the Word, as the eternal days of heaven. His triumph is eternal and universal; and this is a triumph in which his Mother shares. The winter is past, the rain has departed and gone, the flowers of spring appeared on our earth. The time of eternal springtide has radically begun with the resurrection, and we are all invited to share in this joy with Jesus and Mary. But if the flowers have appeared, it is also time for pruning, which means that the wicked and the worthless are separated from the blessed. The resurrection, then, means both joy and grief: joy for the good, grief for the wicked. But the homily ends on a note of pure joy as Mary contemplates and shares in the glory of her Son. The homily is kaleidoscopic, and the images succeed in a variety of patterns which simply cannot be sorted out according to any demonstrably logical order. We begin, after all, at a banquet, and the wine is more than heady. The spirit is one of a joy that goes beyond all telling; a spirit of play, a spirit of improvisation. So, in reading this homily, we would do well to read it in the spirit in which it has obviously been conceived and written down.

Homily VII, on Mary's death and assumption into heaven, begins with a question: Why did Mary not follow Jesus as soon as he ascended into heaven? Why the delay? It was for the sake of the Church, Amadeus explains. For the Apostles in the first instance (how much Mary had to tell them about her Son!); but also as a source of consolation for Christians at large. The Redeemer was now in heaven; but the Mother of the Redeemer was still there as a visible sign of the fulfillment of all that had been promised. Mary's role, then, is ecclesial. Amadeus has a further penetrating insight. He sees Mary's gifts of grace as something contagious. To be close to Mary means to catch something of her purity and faith and humility. This is why she had to remain here below for so long, so that those approaching her could be enkindled from the fire of the Word which filled her, and could breathe the fragrance of the grace of the resurrection which she exhaled. Touching briefly yet again on his preferred theme of Mary the New Eve, Amadeus explains how Mary's prolonged stay on earth, at the very heart of the Church, was a preparation for her glorious reign in heaven. There is a quite remarkable development of this theme, in which Mary is shown as anticipating, even here below, the life of the world to come. The profusion of flowers and scents from the Song of Songs are used to depict the graces which flow from the Virgin Mother to the Church; and from the Church flow to us the rivers of peace and overflowings of grace that have their source in heaven. There is a particularly lovely paragraph, too, on Mary, Queen of peace; for legend had it that the peace inaugurated by the birth of Christ lasted till the death of Mary. All of which, says Amadeus, should answer the question, Why did Mary remain here below after the ascension of her Son? But he gives one further reason for this delay: Mary grows to a beautiful and fruitful old-age as an example and model of perseverance.

The time has come, then, for Mary to follow her Son into glory; and the several pages describing Mary's leave-taking and her Son's reception of her in heaven are as fervent and lyrical as one would expect from a writer such as Amadeus. Without insisting on it, he quite clearly opts for the theological position that Mary is now in heaven body and soul:

There [in heaven], having taken again the substance of her flesh (for it is not lawful to believe that her body saw corruption) and clothed with a double robe, she looks upon God and man in his two natures with a gaze clearer than all others, inasmuch as it is more burning than all, with the eyes of her soul and body.[53]

But Mary continues in heaven the role she began here below in the very heart of the Church; and the homily ends with an assurance that Mary has not forgotten for what purpose she was made Mother of the Redeemer.

Homily VIII is something of a cosmic synthesis. It begins with Mary as the tree sprung from the root of Jesse, spreading its branches over the whole world, and rising so high as to penetrate heaven itself. The fruit of this tree provides nourishment and a perpetual feast for earth and heaven. Several pages are devoted to Amadeus' explicitation of his view that Mary's exaltation and triumph form the obverse side to Satan's fall and defeat. Mary has taken the high place in heaven left vacant by the fall of Lucifer. For all her high estate, however, the Mother of Christ remains very much with us here below. In a particularly penetrating insight, Amadeus gives the reason for Mary's continuing love and concern for us:

The more she beholds from on high the heart of the mighty king the more profoundly she knows, by the grace of divine pity, how to pity the unhappy and to help the afflicted.[54]

This leads into a long, sustained meditation on Mary's mediation. She is the Star of the Sea—though here Amadeus seems to be quite independent of Saint Bernard's splendid development of this theme. She is not content with past triumphs over the enemy, but from heaven continues, at the side of her Son, the battle against sin and the Evil One. But Mary's concern extends to bodies as well as souls, and Amadeus makes explicit reference to miracles of healing wrought in places dedicated to the Mother of God. She is a never-failing source of help and comfort, and her love goes out to saint and sinner alike. The final paragraphs are devoted to the glorious *dénouement* of the whole Mystery of Christ, when, at the Last Judgement, the full meaning of all that has taken place will be made manifest in resplendent light; and the final words of Amadeus are a prayer that we too may find a place in the lovely country of heaven, in the bright resting places of paradise, amid the sparkling fiery jewels of the heavenly Jerusalem.

§

Those who pray the Liturgy of the Hours according to the Roman Rite will have occasion most years to read, as the patristic reading appointed for 22 August, the Memorial of the Queenship of Mary, a lovely passage on Mary, Queen of the world and of peace, excerpted from Amadeus' *Homily VII*. This passage reads well even when taken out of its proper context—a bit like a particularly lovely song excerpted from a Schumann song-cycle. But to appreciate this song to the full, you must hear it in its proper place, with all that comes before and follows: which is why it is a good thing that we now have available a translation of the complete homily-cycle by Amadeus.

Readers familiar with French will find especially helpful the introduction and notes to the Latin-French *Sources chrétiennes* edition.[55] Perhaps even more helpful, however, would be the issue of *Collectanea O.C.R.* 21 (1959), devoted almost in its entirety to articles written on the occasion of the eighth centenary of the death of Saint Amadeus.

Chrysogonus Waddell OCSO

Gethsemani Abbey

NOTES

1. Letter 18, 5; *SBOp* 7:69.
2. Letter 89, 3; ibid., 236-237.
3. J.R.R. Tolkien, *The Return of the King* (New York: Ballantine Books, 1965), p. 285.
4. *Vita Prima auctore Guillelmo* 5, 25; PL 185:241 D.
5. Ibid., 6, 29; PL 185:244 B.
6. Ibid., 7, 33; PL 185:246 C.
7. Translated in *Bernard of Clairvaux: Treatises II* (CF 13). On the chronology of Bernard's early writings, see Damien Van den Eynde, 'Les premiers écrits de S. Bernard,', in ASOC 19 (1963) 189-198; or in Jean Leclercq, *Recueil d'études sur saint Bernard et ses écrits* 3, Storia e letteratura raccolta di studi e testi 114 (Rome: Edizioni di Storia e letteratura, 1969) pp. 343-422.
8. *SBOp* 7:388-392.
9. *SBOp* 5:275-288.
10. *SBOp* 5:228-274.
11. An elenchus of these more occasional marian passages can be found in Gabriele Roschini, *Il Dottore Mariano. Studio sulla dottrina Mariana di S. Bernardo di Chiaravalle nell'VIII centenario del suo glorioso transito* (Rome: Seir-Edizioni Cattoliche, 1953) pp. 26-27.
12. For a particularly profound (though somewhat tangled) study of Saint Bernard's experience of the Bible, see the invaluable study by Maurice Dumontier, *Saint Bernard et la Bible,* Bibliothèque de Spiritualité médiévale (Paris: Desclée de Brouwer, 1953). But for the ultimate in a study of the Saint's recourse to Scripture in the homilies *In Praise of the Virgin Mother,* see the study by Jean Leclercq (in collaboration with J. Figuet), 'La Bible dans les homélies de S. Bernard sur "Missus est",' in *Studi medievali* 5 (1964) 613-648; or in Leclercq, *Recuil* 3, pp. 213-248.
13. *SBOp* 7:388-392. For the date, see Leopold Grill, 'Die angebliche Gegnerschaft des hl. Bernhard von Clairvaux zum Dogma von der unbefleckten Empfängnis Marias,' in ASOC 16 (1960), 60-91, with special reference to pp. 61-65.
14. Letter 174, 2; *SBOp* 7:388-389.
15. *SBOp* 5:275-288.
16. For the pre-bernardine background of this image, see p. 111 of Fr Henri Barré's article, 'Saint Bernard, Docteur Marial', in *Saint Bernard théologien. Actes du Congrès de Dijon, 15-19 septembre, 1953.* ASOC 9 (1953) 92-113.
17. Pp. 113-114 of the translation of the Encyclical Letter of 1953, in Thomas Merton, *The Last of the Fathers. Saint Bernard of Clairvaux and the Encyclical Letter, 'Doctor Mellifluus'* (New York: Harcourt, Brace and Co. 1953).

18.   Barré, p. 113.
19.   *S. Bernardi Vita Prima, Lib. 5 auctore Gaufrido,* c. 2, 15; PL 185: 360 CD.
20.   Ibid., *Lib. 1 auctore Guillelmo,* c. 2, 4; PL 185:299 A-B.
21.   Ibid., 229 A.
22.   A fairly complete anthology of these texts can be found, in French translation, in Pierre Aubron, *L'oeuvre Mariale de Saint Bernard* (Paris: Editions du Cerf-Juvisy, 1935).
23.   This chapter was appended to the Constitution on the Church as a result of the Council vote of October 29, 1963.
24.   See Christine Mohrmann, 'Observations sur la langue et le style de saint Bernard,' used as the introduction to *SBOp* 2 (1958), pp. ix-xxxiii. This analysis is brilliant and definitive. Even more brilliant and insightful, however, is Jean Leclercq's 'Sur le caractère littéraire des sermons de S. Bernard,' first published in *Studi medievali* 7 (1966) 701-744, but later included in Leclercq, *Recueil* 3, pp. 163-210. Fr Leclercq's discussion of the musicality of Bernard's prose is particularly discerning.
25.   See, for instance, Roschini, p. 30, under letter b.
26.   *SBOp* 4:41, lines 21-24.
27.   P. 55 of Fr Dimier's article, 'Les amusements poétiques de saint Bernard,' in *Coll.* 11 (1949) 53-55.
28.   Full details about the history of the text and the establishment of the critical version are in *SBOp* 4:3-11.
29.   The definitive biographical study of our Cistercian bishop is by Fr Anselme Dimier, *Amédée de Lausanne. Disciple de saint Bernard.* Coll. *Figures monastiques* (Abbaye S. Wandrille: Éditions de Fontenelle, 1949). Fr Dimier provides the reader with virtually everything recoverable touching on the life and pastoral activity of Amadeus. The biographical details of our own Introduction are based chiefly on material made accessible by Fr Dimier.
30.   PL 188:1299-1304.
31.   Ibid., col. 1299 B.
32.   Details about the conversion of Amadeus Senior may be found in the annotated edition of the *Vita Amedaei Altae Ripae* by Fr Anselme Dimier, in *Studia Monastica* 5 (1963) 265-304.
33.   Ibid., p. 284.
34.   For complete details on the *cultus* of Amadeus prior to the calendar reforms of Vatican II, see Dimier, *Amédée,* pp. 208-210.
35.   Dimier, *Amédée,* p. 236.
36.   Analyzed in Dimier, *Amédée,* pp. 194-202.
37.   Complete catalogue in Dimier, *Amédée,* pp. 236-239, with texts often given *in extenso* among the many documents included in the Appendix, pp. 257-416.
38.   Dimier, *Amédée,* pp. 241-243.
39.   PL 188:1303-1346.
40.   Amédée de Lausanne, *Huit homélies mariales* SCh 72 (Paris: Editions du Cerf, 1960).
41.   Description in SCh 72, pp. 46-47.
42.   Ibid., p. 47.
43.   Ibid., pp. 47-48.
44.   Complete listing of printed editions in SCh 72, pp. 48-49; or Dimier, *Amédée,* pp. 235-236.
45.   The history of translations is limited to French translations, and is given in the pages indicated in the preceding note; to which should be added, of course, the translation by Dom Antoine Dumas, prepared precisely for the *Sources chrétiennes* edition.
46.   *Collectanea* 21 (1959) 29-62.

47.   P. 105.
48.   SCh 72, p. 13.
49.   P. 104.
50.   PL 189:673-674.
51.   P. 96.
52.   P. 101.
53.   P. 127.
54.   P. 131.
55.   Above, note 40.

IN PRAISE OF THE VIRGIN MOTHER

FOUR HOMILIES

BY

BERNARD OF CLAIRVAUX

PREFACE

MY DEVOTION has been urging me to write something but so far business has hindered me. Now that sickness prevents me from joining the brothers in community, however, I do not want to waste what little bit of leisure I can snatch during the night by depriving myself of sleep. I think it a good idea therefore to attempt something about which I have often thought but which is extremely difficult: to say something in praise of the Virgin Mother based on the gospel reading in which Luke tells the story of the Lord's annunciation. Even though there is no real need for me to write this for the brothers' spiritual progress—which must always be my first concern—and even though there does not seem to be any immediate use for such an undertaking, nevertheless, as long as it in no way prevents me from being at their service, it seems to me they ought not to take it amiss if I satisfy my own devotion.

HOMILY I

THE ANGEL GABRIEL WAS SENT BY GOD
TO A CITY OF GALILEE NAMED NAZA-
RETH, TO A VIRGIN ENGAGED TO A MAN
WHOSE NAME WAS JOSEPH, OF THE
HOUSE OF DAVID. AND THE VIRGIN'S
NAME WAS MARY.* And so on.   *Lk 1:26-27

W E MAY WONDER what the Evangelist's
intention was when he made such speci-
fic mention of so many proper names.
I think he wanted to be sure we should not give care-
less hearing to what he was going to take such care
to narrate. You notice that he mentions the messenger who was sent, the Lord by whom he was
sent, the virgin to whom he was sent and the virgin's
fiancé. He even mentions by name their race, the city
they came from, and the district.

Why? Do you suppose that any of these details
were set down without a good reason? Of course
not! If no leaf can fall from a tree without cause*   *Mt 10:29
and not a single sparrow fall to the ground without
the heavenly Father's knowledge,* am I to think that   *Mt 6:26
a superfluous word could fall from the lips of the
holy Evangelist—especially in recording the sacred
history of the Word? I think not.* All his words, if   *Lk 17:10
only they have a diligent reader (one who know how
to suck honey out of the rock and oil out of the
hardest stone),* contain supernal mysteries and are   *Deut 32:13
full of heavenly sweetness. Now in those days the

5

*Joel 3:18
*Ex 3:17

*Is 45:8
†Is 35:2
*Ps 85:12
*Ps 68:15
*Ps 85:10

*Ps 42:6

*Job 37:17
*Mal 4:2
*Sg 4:16
*Ps 147:18

*2 Cor 4:6

*Ps 19:10

*Lk 1:26
*2 Cor 5:20

*1 Cor 1:24

mountains dripped with sweet wine* and the hills flowed with milk and honey;* then the heavens dropped dew from above and the clouds showered the Just One,* causing the earth to open out and, rejoicing, to blossom forth the Saviour.† The Lord showed his kindness and our earth bore its fruit.* On the holiest of mountains, God's chosen dwelling,* righteousness and peace kissed each other.* Then too the holy Evangelist, himself one of the mountains—and by no means the least*—made known to us in words flowing like honey the beginning of our salvation, so long desired. It was as if a gentle southerly wind were blowing* and as if the Sun of righteousness were shining close to earth,* causing sweet smelling spiritual spices to flow.* Oh if only God would send forth his word to melt us.* Oh if only his Spirit would inspire us that we might understand the gospel words. Oh if only they could become for our hearts* more desireable than gold, even than the most precious stone, and sweeter than honey and the honeycomb.*

2. The Evangelist writes: 'The angel Gabriel was sent by God.'* I do not think that Gabriel was one of the lesser angels, one of those ambassadors* usually sent to earth to handle affairs. I deduce this from his name, which means *God's fortitude,* and also from the fact that he was sent by God himself and not, as it sometimes happens, by some more important angel. This is why he says 'by God'. Or he may have said 'by God' lest anyone imagine that, even before making his plan known to the Virgin, God had revealed it to some of the holy spirits apart from the archangel Gabriel who, because he was superior to the others, was considered worthy to bear so great a name and so great a message. The angel's name is in harmony with his message. Who could better be suited to announce Christ, the very Power of God,* than someone who had the honor of being called by a like name? For what is fortitude if not power? There is nothing unbecoming or out of place for the messenger to have the same name as his Lord,

because though they both bear this name, they do so for very different reasons. Christ is called the fortitude or power of God in one sense and the angel in another. The angel is the power of God merely nominally, whereas Christ is so essentially. He is like that more powerful man who overcame the strong keeping his household in peace by force of arms* *Lk 11:21-23
and, taking his arms away [Christ] powerfully wrested from him the spoils of captivity. The angel is called the fortitude of God either in function of his office, which was to announce the coming of Power, or perhaps because he was to comfort a virgin, timid, simple and modest by nature, so that she should neither be afraid nor tremble at the novelty of this miracle. He did that when he said 'Fear not, Mary, you have found grace with God'.* Nor is it un- *Lk 1:30
reasonable to suppose, though the Evangelist does say so, that it was this same angel who comforted her fiancé,* a man no less humble and god-fearing. *Lk 2:25
'Joseph, son of David,' he said, 'do not be afraid to take Mary as your wife.'* Gabriel was fittingly *Mt 1:20
chosen for this mission. Perhaps it would be better to say that he had the right to so great a name because he was to carry out so great a mission.

3. 'The angel Gabriel was sent by God.' Where? 'Into a city of Galilee called Nazareth.'* Like *Lk 1:26
Nathanael, we might well wonder whether anything good can come from Nazareth.* Nazareth means *Jn 1:46
flower. It seems to me that the heavenly promises which were made to the patriarchs Abraham, Isaac and Jacob* were some sort of seed of divine knowl- *Gen 50:23
edge cast down, so to speak, from heaven to earth, the seed of which it is written: 'If the Lord God of hosts had not left us a seed, we should have been like Sodom and reduced like Gomorrha.'* This seed *Rom 9:29
flowered* first in the wonderful doings† which were *Is 17:11
shown forth in symbols** and in riddles†† as Israel †Ps 78:32
came out of Egypt,§ all along the way‡ through **1 Cor 10:62
the desert* to the Land of Promise,† and afterwards ††1 Cor 13:12
in the visions and foretellings of the Prophets, in the §Ps 114:1
setting up of the kingdom and the priesthood, even ‡Ps 68:4
*Neh 9:19
†Heb 11:9

until Christ's coming. Not without reason do we understand Christ to be the fruit of the flowers sprung from this seed, for David says, 'The Lord will look with kindness upon the earth and it shall bear fruit'.* And again, 'I will place the fruit of your womb upon your throne.'* It was at Nazareth† therefore that Christ's birth was first announced, because in the flower lies the hope of fruit to come. But once the fruit is formed, the flower fades.* When Truth appeared in flesh and blood, the figure passed away.* So it is that Nazareth is called a city of Galilee,* which means 'passing over'. Because once Christ had been born, every one of the events passed away to which we have referred above and which, as the Apostle says, 'happened to them as a sign'.* We too, now that we have the Fruit, realize that the flowers have faded. Even as we watched them blossoming we foresaw that they would fade because, David says, 'they are like a dream, like grass which springs up fresh each morning. In the morning it flourishes and is fresh, but in the evening it fades and withers.'* *In the evening* means when the fulness of time had come,* when God sent his only-begotten Son, made of a woman and subject to the Law; he who said of himself 'behold, I make all things new'.* It was then that the old passed away* and disappeared, just as flowers fade and wither in the newness of ripening fruit.* Again, it is written, 'the grass withers, the flower fades, but the word of our God endures for ever'.* I think no one doubts that the Word is the fruit, and the Word is Christ.

4. Christ then is the good Fruit* which endures for ever. But where is the withered grass and the faded flower? The prophet tells us 'all flesh is grass and all its beauty is like the flower of the fields.'* If all flesh is grass, then the carnal people of Jewry were also grass. And while this people clung to the parched written code and were drained of spiritual sweetness, was the grass not withering? And when they boasted* in the Law, after this had been done away with, did the flower not also fade? If the flower has not faded,

*Ps 85:12
*Ps 132:11
†Mt 2:24

*Is 40:7

*1 Cor 7:31
*Lk 1:26

*1 Cor 10:11

*Ps 90:5-6
*Gal 4:4

*Rev 21:5
*2 Cor 5:17

*Rom 6:4,
  Mt 4:7
*Is 40:8

*Mt 7:17

*Is 40:6

*Rom 2:23

what then has become of the kingdom, the priesthood, the prophets, and the temple? What has
become of all those wonderful things about which
they used to boast and brag; 'the things that we have
heard and seen, things that our fathers have told
us'?* What of those things of which they once said, *Ps 77:3
'He appointed a law in Israel which he commanded
our fathers to teach to their children'?* All these *Ps 77:5
thoughts come to mind in connection with the
words 'to a city of Galilee named Nazareth'.* *Lk 1:26

5. Into that particular city, then, the angel Gabriel
was sent by God.* To whom? 'To a virgin engaged to *Lk 1:26
a man whose name was Joseph.'* Who is this virgin *Lk 1:27
noble enough to be greeted by an angel and yet
humble enough to be the fiancé of a workman?

How gracious is this union of virginity and
humility! A soul in whom humility embellishes virginity and virginity ennobles humility finds no little
favor with God. Imagine then how much more
worthy of reverence must she have been whose
humility was raised by motherhood and whose
virginity consecrated by her childbearing. You are
told that she is a virgin. You are told that she is
humble. If you are not able to imitate the virginity
of this humble maid, then imitate the humility of
the virgin maid. Virginity is a praiseworthy virtue,
but humility is by far the more necessary. The one is
only counselled; the other is demanded. To the first
you have been invited; to the second you are obliged.
Concerning the first he said, 'he who is able to
receive this, let him receive it';* of the second is said, *Mt 19:12
'Truly I said to you, unless you become like this little
child, you will not enter the kingdom of heaven'.* *Mt 18:3
The first is rewarded; the second is required. You can
be saved without virginity; without humility you
cannot be. Humility which deplores the loss of virginity can still find favor. Yet I dare say that without
humility not even Mary's virginity would have been
acceptable. The Lord says, 'Upon whom shall my
Spirit rest, if not upon him that is humble and
contrite in spirit?'* *On the humble,* he says, not *Is 66:2

on the virgin. Had Mary not been humble, then, the Holy Spirit would not have rested upon her. Had he not rested upon her, she would not have become pregnant. How indeed could she have conceived by him* without him? It seems evident then that she conceived by the Holy Spirit* because, as she herself said, God 'regarded the humility of his handmaiden'* rather than her virginity. And even if it was because of her virginity that she found favor, she conceived nevertheless on account of her humility. Thus there is no doubt that her virginity was found pleasing because her humility made it so.

*Lk 1:31
*Lk 1:35
*Lk 1:48

6. What have you to say to that, haughty virgin? Mary, making no account of her virginity, was happy in her humility. Yet you, heedless of humility, preen yourself on your virginity? 'God has regarded the humility of his handmaiden,' she says.* Who is she? A holy virgin, if ever there was one! A sober virgin, a devout virgin. Would you be more chaste than she? More devout? Do you fancy that your modesty is so much more pleasing than Mary's chastity that you on your own can do without the humility she needed to find favor with God? If so, to the extent that you are more worthy of respect because you have received a singular gift of chastity, you do yourself more harm,* because you tarnish its beauty by the adulteration of pride.

*Lk 1:48

*Prov 9:7

It is better* for you not to be a virgin than to be puffed up over your virginity. Not everyone is a virgin, but there are still fewer who to virginity join humility. So if you can do no more than admire Mary's virginity, try to imitate her humility and for you this will be enough.* But if you are both a virgin and humble, then whoever you are, you are great.

*Mt 5:29

*2 Cor 12:9

7. But in Mary there is something else still more admirable; her childbearing allied with her virginity. Never since the world began* has it been known for any woman to be at once a mother and a virgin. If you just think whose mother she is surely you must

*Jn 9:32

be astounded at such marvellous greatness. Who
could ever admire this enough? To your way of
thinking, or rather, not yours but Truth's, should she
not be exalted above all the choirs of angels, she
who bore God the Son? Who else would dare, as Mary
did, to call 'son' the Lord and God of angels and to
say 'son, why have you treated us so?'* Would any   *Lk 2:48*
angel dare this? They already consider it a great
favor to be called, and to be, angels, when they are
no more than spirits, as David suggests when he says
He makes the spirits his angels.* Yet his was the   *Ps 104:4*
same Majesty whom they serve with awe and
reverence* that Mary, knowing herself the mother,   *Heb 12:28*
confidently called her son. Nor did God disdain
to be called what he had deigned to become. As the
Evangelist tells us a bit later, 'he was obedient to
them'.* Who? God. To whom? To men. God, I   *Lk 2:51*
repeat, to whom the angels are subject, he whom the
principalities and the power obey,* he was obedient   *Col 2:15*
to Mary. And not only to Mary but to Joseph, too,
for Mary's sake. Marvel then at these two things: the
gracious kindness of the Son and the surpassing dignity of the mother. Choose which you consider more
wonderful. Just imagine! Double marvel! God does
what a woman says—unheard of humility. A woman
outranks God—unparalleled sublimity. In praise of the
virgins we sing that 'they follow the Lamb wherever
he goes'.* Of what praise then do you consider her   *Rev 14:4*
worthy, who preceded him?

8. Man, learn to obey! Earth, learn to be subject!
Dust, I say, learn to submit yourself! The Evangelist
tells you that your Creator was obedient to them*—   *Lk 2:51*
meaning to Mary and Joseph, of course. Blush for
shame, proud ash. God stoops down in humility, and
you exalt yourself? God is obedient to men, and you,
anxious to lord it over men, set yourself up as your
own authority? God preserve me from ever thinking
such a thing! And if I should, may he be so kind as to
rebuke me with that answer he gave to the apostle:
'Get behind me, Satan! You do not know the things
of God.'* Every time I seek to lord it over men, I am   *Mt 16:23*

trying to get in front of my God—and then, in all
truth, I do not know the things of God. For it was

Lk 2:51

said of him that he was obedient to them.*

O man, if it is beneath your dignity to follow the
example of a man, surely it will not be beneath you
to follow your Creator. Maybe you can no longer

Rev 14:4

follow him wherever he goes,* but condescend at
least to follow him where he stooped for you. That is
to say, if you cannot follow the high road of
virginity, at least take the sure road of humility. If
anyone, even a virgin, should turn aside from this
strait way, it seems evident to me that he does not

Rev 14:4

follow the Lamb wherever he goes.*

A defiled but humble person can follow the Lamb,
as can a haughty virgin, but neither follows him
wherever he goes. The one cannot reach up to the
purity of the spotless Lamb and the other will not
deign to stoop to the gentleness by which he was

Is 53:7

dumb not only before the shearer* but even before
the slayer. Moreover, the sinner's path of humility is
safer than the haughty virgin's way. Making amends
humbly purifies the one's impurity, while pride defiles
the other's chastity.

9. Blessed Mary! She lacks neither humility nor
virginity. And what unique virginity. Motherhood did
not stain but honored it. What extraordinary humility.
Fruitful virginity did not tarnish but exalted it. And
matchless fruitfulness went hand in hand with both
virginity and humility. Which of them is not wonderful? Which is not incomparable? Which is not unique?
I should not be at all surprised if, having meditated
upon them, you hesitated to say which you find
more praiseworthy, whether you think more amazing
the fruitfulness in the virgin or the integrity in the
mother; nobility in child-bearing or, in spite of such
nobility, humility. Possibly it is more excellent to
have all three together than to have one of them
alone. For there is no doubt that she who was thus
thrice blessed was more blessed than if she had
received only one of them. And yet, is it so extraordinary that God whom we read and see to be

wonderful in his saints,* should show himself even more wonderful in his mother? *Ps 68:35

You who are married, then, reverence the integrity of her flesh amid frail flesh. And you, consecrated virgins, admire the virgin's fruitfulness. Let all strive to imitate the humility of the Mother of God. Holy angels, revere the mother of your King, and you who worship our humble virgin's child, for he is your King and ours, the restorer of our race, the builder of your city. Angels, allow us men to join with you in singing worthy praise of his highness and his lowliness, he who with you is so sublime and yet with us so humble. To him be honor and glory for evermore. Amen.* *Rom 16:27

HOMILY II

THE NEW SONG* which only virgins will have   *Rev 14:3*
the right to sing in the kingdom of God will
certainly be sung by the Queen of Virgins and
she will surely be the first to intone it. Furthermore,
I think that she will not only sing in unison with the
virgin choir, as I have said, but that she will gladden
the city of God* with an even sweeter and more   *Ps 46:4*
charming hymn, one whose melodious sound* no   *Wis 17:18*
virgin, however worthy, could either sing or intone,
but her who glories in childbirth, divine childbirth.
She glories I have said, in childbirth not for itself, but
in him whom she has borne. God, for it was God
indeed whom she bore, having it in mind to give his
mother special glory in heaven, was careful to prepare her on earth with a special grace; whereby she
conceived undefiled beyond all telling and unspoiled
she gave birth. Only this mode of birth was becoming
to God—to be born of a virgin. The only childbearing
becoming to a virgin is to give birth to God alone.*   *Ps 62:1*
So it was that the Maker of mankind,* in order to   *Is 17:7*
become man, born of human flesh, had to choose*   *Sir 45:16*
one person out of all the living, or rather, he had to
create someone whom he knew would be worthy*   *Wis 6:16*
to be his mother, someone in whom he was sure he
could delight.* That was why he wanted her to be a   *Mal 3:1*
virgin, someone unstained from whom he himself
could be born stainless, for he was to wipe away all
our stains.* He wanted her to be humble as well,   *Jn 1:29*
someone of whom he could himself be born gentle
and humble of heart,* because he intended to give all   *Mt 11:29*
mankind the necessary and most beneficial example

of these virtues. So he now gave the blessing of child-birth to the virgin in whom he had first inspired the vow of virginity and from whom he had first demanded humility. Had it been otherwise, that is, had there been in her any good, however slight, which was not a gift of grace, how could the angel have proclaimed her full of grace in the terms he does?*

*Lk 1:28

2. So that she might conceive and give birth to the Holy of Holies,* she was made holy in her body by the gift of virginity and she accepted that gift of humility to become holy in spirit too. This queenly maiden,* adorned with the jewels of these virtues, radiant with this perfect beauty* of spirit and body, renowned in the assembly of the Most High* for her loveliness and her beauty,* so ravished the eyes† of all the heavenly citizens that the heart of the King himself desired her beauty* and sent down to her from on high a heavenly messenger. And this is what the Evangelist is telling us here when he states that an angel was sent from God to a virgin.* He says *from God to a virgin;* from the highest to the humble; from the Master to the handmaiden; from the Creator to the creature! How kind God is! How matchless is the Virgin! Make haste,* mothers and daughters, hasten all you who after Eve and because of Eve were born and do yourselves give birth in pain. Gather round this virginal chamber and, if you can, enter your sister's* chaste inner room.† Behold, God has sent down for the Virgin. Behold, Mary is being spoken for* by the angel. Put your ear to the door,* strain to listen to the tidings he brings.† Maybe you will hear soothing words to comfort you.*

*Dan 9:24

*Song 7:1
*Esther 15:5
*Sir 24:2
*Ps 44:5
†Judith 16:9

*Ps 45:11

*Lk 1:26-27

*Sg 8:14

*Sg 8:8
†Wis 17:4

*Sg 8:8
*Sir 21:24
†Sg 8:13

*Est 15:8

3. Rejoice, Adam, our father, and you more especially, mother Eve, exult. You were the parents of mankind and the destroyers* of mankind and, most wretchedly, our destroyers even before you were our parents. Now let both of you, I say, take consolation in your daughter, and in so great a

*Zeph 9:27

daughter, especially you, woman, from whom evil had its beginning,* you whose reproach has been handed down to all womankind. The time has now come for this reproach to be taken away. No longer will man have any reason to accuse woman as he did long ago when, attempting cravenly* to excuse himself, he did not hesitate cruelly to accuse her saying, 'The woman whom you gave to be with me, she gave me the fruit of the tree and I ate it'.* Eve, run then to Mary, run to your daughter. Let your daughter now plead* for her mother and take away her mother's reproach. Let her now reconcile her mother to the Father. For if man fell on account of woman, surely he will rise only through another woman. What was it you said, Adam? 'The woman whom you gave to be with me, she gave me the fruit of the tree, and I ate.'* What evil words! Far from excusing you, they condemn you.* However, Wisdom prevails against evil.* The occasion for pardon which God endeavored to draw from you by his cross-examination, but could not, he found in the treasure of his never-failing kindness.* Yes, he gave woman for woman: a wise one for a foolish one;* a humble one for an arrogant one.* Instead of the tree of death, she offers you a taste of life; in place of the poisonous fruit of bitterness she holds out to you the sweetness of eternity's fruit. Change your words of evil excuse into a song of thanksgiving then and say, 'Lord, the woman whom you gave to be with me, she gave me the fruit of the tree of life, and I ate; and it was sweeter than honey to my mouth,* for by it have you given me life'. Behold, for this was the angel sent to a virgin. O Virgin maid, admirable and worthy of all our honor.* O uniquely venerable woman! O fairest among all women!* You have repaired your parents' weakness, and restored life* to all their offspring.

4. 'The angel was sent', he says, 'to a Virgin',* a virgin in her body, a virgin in her spirit, a virgin by profession, a virgin such as the Apostle describes, holy in spirit and body.* Nor was this virgin discovered at the last minute, as if by chance. She was

*Sir 25:33

*Wis 17:11

*Gen 3:12

*Hos 2:2

*Gen 3:12
*Wis 17:11
*Wis 7:30

*Sir 30:23
*Mt 25:2
*1 Cor 5:2

*Ps 119:103

*Sg 7:6
*Sg 5:9
*Ruth 4:15

*Lk 1:26-27

*1 Cor 7:34

chosen ages ago. The Most High foreknew her and
prepared her for himself. She was preserved by the
angels, prefigured by the patriarchs, promised by the
Jn 7:52   prophets. Search the Scriptures* and verify what I
am saying.

Do you want me to bring in still other witnesses?
Let me mention just a few among the many. Whom
else do you imagine God had in mind when he said to
the serpent, 'I will put enmity between you and the
Gen 3:14-15   woman'?* And if you still doubt whether or not he
was speaking of Mary, listen to the next words, 'She
Gen 3:15   shall bruise your head'.* To whom would such
victory be reserved if not to Mary? It is obvious that
it was she who bruised this venemous head, for she
Ps 108:13   brought to nothing* all suggestions of the evil one,
those of carnal lust as well as those of spiritual pride.

5. Whom else was Solomon looking for when he
Prov 31:10   said, 'Who shall find a valiant woman?'* That wise
Ex 36:1   man* was well acquainted with the weakness of this
sex, frail in body and fickle in mind. But because he
Gen 3:15   had read God's promise* that he who had prevailed
over woman would in turn be prevailed over by her,
and realizing that this was only right, he exclaimed,
Judith 15:1   greatly amazed:* 'Who shall find a valiant woman?'
This is to say: if the salvation of all of us, the resti-
tution of our innocence and the victory over the
Judith 16:1   enemy hang upon the hand of a woman,* it becomes
very necessary indeed that he foresee that she be
equal to so great a task. Yet, 'who shall find a
valiant woman?' For fear that we should think that
he had searched hopelessly, he goes on in a prophetic
Prov 31:10   vein: 'Her price is beyond that of anything afar.'*
This means that her price is neither cheap nor low
nor mediocre. The price of this valiant woman is not
Job 28:13   known to man* on earth but is found in the heights
Sir 1:3   of heaven,* and not even in the heavens† nearest the
†*Sir 1:5*   earth, but, in the very heaven of heavens.*
Ps 19:6   That bush which Moses in days past saw shooting
Ex 3:2   forth flames and yet not burning away,* what did it
signify if not Mary giving birth and yet not suffering
Rev 12:2   the pangs of birth?* What, I ask, did Aaron's rod,

which blossomed without being watered,* portend if
not Mary who conceived although she knew no man?
The even greater mystery of this great miracle Isaiah
taught us when he said: 'There shall come forth a
shoot from the rod of Jesse, and a blossom shall grow
out of its roots.'* The rod symbolized the Virgin and
the blossom the virgin birth.

6. But perhaps you consider this interpretation
(which makes Christ out to be the blossom) in
contradiction with the passage further up where he
was designated not by the rod's blossom, but by the
blossom's fruit. If so, you should realize that this same
rod of Aaron* not only blossomed but also put forth
leaves and bore fruit, and that Christ was symbolized
not only by the blossom and fruit but by the leaves as
well. You realize that in the case of the rod of
Moses,* Christ was figured by neither fruit nor
blossom, but by the rod itself. It was with the rod he
was carrying that Moses once struck the waters to
divide them to provide a crossing, and once brought
forth waters from the rock for drinking.* I find no
difficulty in these different things figuring Christ in
his various aspects. In the rod we recognize his
power, in the blossom his fragrant perfume* and
in the fruit the sweetness of his savor.* By the
foliage is signified that vigilant protection by which he
never fails to cover those little ones* who run to
shelter under the shadow of his wings,* to escape
either the burning heat of carnal desires* or the face
of the wicked who oppress them.* How good and
desirable is the shadow* beneath the wings of
Jesus! There is a snug haven for all who flee to him,*
sweet repose for the weary. Be merciful to me, Lord
Jesus, be merciful to me, for my soul trusts in you and
in the shadow of your wings will I hope until iniquity has passed by.* In the witness brought forward
by Isaiah,* however, take the blossom to mean the
Son and the rod his mother, for as the rod blossomed without seed, so the Virgin conceived without
man.* Nor did the sacred childbearing of the Virgin
do more harm to her chastity than did the blossoming

*Num 17:8

*Is 11:1

*Num 17:8

*Ex 14:16

*Ex 17:6

*Sg 1:3
*Wis 16:20

*Mk 10:14
*Ps 17:8
*1 Pet 2:11
*Ps 17:9
*Sg 2:3
*Ps 143:9

*Ps 57:1
*Is 11:1

*Is 7:14

of the rod to its greenness.

7. Let us bring in other scriptural witnesses applicable to the virgin mother and God her son. Gideon's fleece,* for example, which having been shorn from the flesh without drawing blood was laid on the threshing floor, where dew dropped down once on the wool alone and then only on the ground around—could it symbolize anything except that flesh which was taken from the Virgin's flesh without harm being done to her virginity? When the heavens dropped down from above* the fullness of the divine nature poured itself on her,* from which fullness we have all received,* and without which we are nothing but dry land.* Gideon's action seems to fit in quite prettily with the prophet's words where he says: 'May he come down like rain upon the fleece.'* The words which follow these—'and as showers pattering upon the earth'*—signify exactly the same thing as did the threshing floor when it was discovered soaked with dew. This abundant rain* which God had stored up for his inheritance fell with hushed silence into the virgin womb, penetrating her gently without the din* of human intervention. In later times, however, it was broadcast over all the earth by the mouths of preachers. Then it was no longer like dew falling upon fleece, but like showers pattering down upon the earth,* accompanied by the din of words and resonance of miracles. The rainbearing clouds* were mindful of the orders they had received when they were sent forth: 'What I tell you in the dark, utter in the light; and what you hear whispered, proclaim from the house-tops.'* That was what they did, for, 'Their sound has gone out into all lands, and their words to the end of the world'.*

8. Let us listen also to Jeremiah prophesying. Full of ardent desire for one who was still to come and confidently promising one whom he could not yet point out among us, he added new [prophecy] to old, saying: 'The Lord has created a new thing on earth: a woman shall enclose a man.'* Who is this

*Jg 6:37-40

*Ps 68:9
*Col 2:9
*Jn 1:16
*Wis 19:7

*Ps 72:6

*Ibid.

*Ps 68:9

*I Cor 13:1

*Ps 72:6
*Qo 11:3

*Mt 10:27

*Ps 19:4

*Jer 31:22

woman? Who is this man? And if he is a man, how
can he be enclosed by a woman? Or if he can be
enclosed by a woman, how is he a man? To speak
more plainly, how can he be a man and be in his
mother's womb?* For that is what being enclosed   *Jn 3:4*
by a woman means. We know that men pass through
infancy, childhood, adolescence and young manhood and come to a ripe old age. Who then, once he
has grown up, can be enclosed by a woman? If the
prophet had said, 'A woman encloses an infant', or
'A woman encloses a babe', there would be nothing
new or wonderful about that. But we have something
quite different here, since the prophet speaks of 'a
man'. So let us go into this novelty which God has
created on earth: a woman enclosing a man, and a
man folding up his limbs within a woman's frail little
body. What can this miracle be? As Nicodemus
asked, 'Can a man enter a second time into his
mother's womb and be born anew?'*   *Jn 3:4*

9. Perhaps if I direct my attention to this virginal
conception, this holy birth, I shall discover among
the many new and marvelous things to be seen
by one who searches diligently* this very novelty   'Mt 2:7-8
which I cited from the prophet. In it one recognizes
short length,* narrow breadth,† lowly height, level   *Eph 3:8
depth. There one perceives an unshining light, a dumb †Rom 8:39
word, parched water, famished bread. And, if you
look carefully, you will see power being ruled, wisdom being taught, strength being borne up; God
suckling but giving bread to angels; God crying, but
comforting the unhappy. If you look carefully you
will see sad joy, timorous trust, ailing health, inani-
mate life, frail strength. But you will also see, which
is just as amazing, sadness giving joy, fear giving comfort, pain healing, death vivifying, weakness fortify-
ing. Surely, then, I shall also discover that very marvel
for which I am looking. Surely, among all these
[paradoxes] when you see Mary bearing in her
womb Jesus, the man approved by God, you cannot
fail to recognize the woman enclosing a man.* For I   *Acts 2:22
would have said that Jesus was a man not only when

*Lk 24:19
*Sg 8:1
*Lk 2:52
*1 Cor 14:20
*Bar 3:26
*Lk 2:7
*Lk 2:42
*2 Mac 5:24
†Dan 11:33
*Lk 4:1
*Is 11:2-3
*Lk 2:52
*Lk 2:43

he was called a prophet mighty in deed and word,* but even when his mother was nursing at her gentle breast* the tender limbs of the infant God or keeping him safe within her womb. Even before his birth, Jesus was a man, not in age of course, but in wisdom;* not by the vigor of his body, but in his soul, by the maturity of his thinking* rather than the greatness of his stature.* Nor did Jesus have any less wisdom, or rather he was not less Wisdom, when he was conceived than when he was born, when he was little than when he was grown up. Thus, whether he was lying hidden within the womb* or crying in the manger, whether he was a stripling youth asking the teachers questions in the Temple,* or a grown man* teaching the people,† he was always equally filled with the Holy Spirit.* There was never any moment whatever of his age when that fullness which he assumed at the instant of his conception in the womb was in any way diminished or augmented. He was perfect from the beginning. From the very beginning, I tell you, he was filled with the spirit of wisdom and understanding, the spirit of counsel and fortitude, the spirit of knowledge and piety and the spirit of the fear of the Lord.*

10. Do not be troubled by what you read of him in that other passage: 'Jesus increased in wisdom and stature and in grace with God and man'.* What is said here about his wisdom and his grace are to be understood not as what was but as what appeared to be. That is to say, he never acquired anything new which he did not previously possess. He only appeared to acquire it when he wanted it to appear. You, men, you do not develop when and as you wish. Your development is regulated and your life arranged without your being aware of it. But the boy Jesus* who arranges your life, also arranged his own, and he appeared wise when and to whom he willed, still wiser when and to whom he willed, and extremely wise when and to whom he willed, though actually he was never anything in himself but extremely wise. In the same way, just as he was always full of grace

both with God and men, as became him, he at his
own choosing manifested sometimes more and sometimes less according to the measure that he knew to
be in harmony with the merits of those around him
or useful for their salvation. It seems obvious then
that Jesus had the mind of a man even though he had
not always appeared a man in body.* Furthermore,   *Is 53:2*
why should I doubt that he was already a man when
in the womb, when I do not hesitate to acknowledge
that he was God there? Surely it is less great to be
man than to be God?

11. But let us see whether what Isaiah says about
Aaron's new blossoms,* mentioned further up, will   *Num 17:8*
shed full light on this novelty of Jeremiah's. Isaiah
says, 'Behold, a young woman shall conceive and
bear a son.'* Here you have the younger woman, the   *Is 7:14*
virgin maid. Do you also want to hear who the man
is? The prophet goes on: 'She shall call his name
Emmanuel',* that is, God among us. Thus, the   *Is 7:14*
woman enclosing a man is the Virgin conceiving
God. Do you notice how beautifully and harmoni-
ously the marvellous deeds and the mystic words of
the Holy Scriptures agree? You see what an extraordinary miracle is accomplished in and through the
Virgin! A miracle which so many other miracles
anticipated, so many oracles promised. One and the
same spirit* moved the Prophets and although they   *1 Cor 14:32*
used differing signs at different times, they foretold
and foresaw the same event in many and various
ways,* but not by a varying spirit. What was shown   *Heb 1:1*
to Moses in the bush and fire,* to Aaron in the rod   *Ex 3:2*
and blossom, to Gideon in the fleece and dew,
Solomon perceived clearly in the valiant woman and
her price. Jeremiah prophesied it even more clearly
when he mentioned the protection which a woman
gave to a man. Isaiah was the most explicit of all
when he spoke about the Virgin and God, and the
Angel Gabriel by his greeting made it known to the
Virgin herself.* For it is she of whom the Evangelist *Lk 1:28*
writes when he says, 'The Angel Gabriel was sent
from God to a virgin engaged to Joseph'.*   *Lk 1:26-27*

12. 'To a Virgin engaged . . . . ' Why 'engaged'?
I tell you, and have explained, because she was a
chosen virgin destined to conceive, a virgin who was
to give birth to a child. It seems surprising that she
was engaged when she was not destined for marriage.
Could this be mere coincidence? No, it is not acci-
dental; there is a reason for it. Everything was
thought out as a very useful and necessary device.
Everything happened in keeping with the divine
plan. Allow me to give you my opinion on the
matter, or rather not mine but that of the Fathers
before me. Mary's engagement is to be explained in
the same way as Thomas's doubting. It was the custom among the Jews for a bride to be given into the
custody of her bridegroom from the day of her
Sg 3:11 betrothal* until the time for the wedding. In this
way he was able to watch over her purity with even
greater care so that they might come together all the
more faithfully. Thus, just as Thomas putting out
Jn 20:25 his hand in doubt to touch the Lord* was to become
a stout witness to his resurrection, so Joseph, in
engaging himself to Mary, watched over her reputation by his protection and thus became the faithful
witness to her modesty. Thomas's doubt and Mary's
engagement fit beautifully together. In both instances
we risk being trapped in the snare of a similar mistake
over his faith and her purity and into thinking our
suspicion justified. But, by means of very prudent
and kind workings, things turn out quite to the
contrary, so that any lurking suspicion is swept
away and certainly made fast. And sure enough I,
weak man that I am, I find it easier to believe in the
Son's resurrection when I see Thomas doubtfully
touching him than when I see Cephas believing on
simple hearsay. Likewise, I have more faith in the
mother's purity when I know that her fiancé watched
over and witnessed it than I would if the Virgin
2 Cor 1:12 defended herself solely by her own conscience.*
Tell me, I say, who knowing her to be unwedded and
yet pregnant would not suspect her of being a harlot
rather than a virgin? And it would not do at all for
such a thing to be rumored about the Mother of our

Lord. It was more honorable and more honest for it
to be thought for a time that Christ had been born in
wedlock than that he was the child of unlawful
union.*

Wis 4:6

13. 'But', you object, 'could not God have given
some sure sign which would have preserved his
earthly origin from infamous suspicion and his
mother from shame?' Yes, he could have done so, but
he could not have kept secret from the demons what
was known openly to men. It was only fitting that
the mystery of his divine plan* should momentarily

Judith 2:2

be hidden from the prince of this world,* not

Jn 12:31

because God needed to fear his interference had he
chosen to make it known openly,* but because

Sir 39:11

He who does whatever he will not only by power but
also by wisdom is accustomed to observe a certain
harmony in events and times throughout all his
works, for the sake of the beauty of order. That is
why in this the most wonderful of all his works, our
redemption, he wanted to manifest not only his
power but his prudence as well. It pleased him to
reconcile man to himself in the same way and by the
means that had caused him to fall—though, of
course, God could have accomplished it any other
way he wished. Just as the devil deceived the woman
first and then overcome man through the woman, so
now he was going to be led astray by a virgin woman
and later be vanquished openly by the man Christ. In
this way the workings of devotion would cheat evil
deceit, the power of Christ would overcome the
force of the evil one, God would be seen to be wiser
and stronger than the devil. Nothing could be more
becoming than that Wisdom incarnate should prevail
over spiritual evil.* In this way not only did he reach

Wis 7:30

mightily from one end of the earth to the other, but
he also ordered all things pleasingly.* He reached out

Wis 8:1

from one end of the earth to the other, from heaven
to the pit of hell. 'If I ascend to heaven,' it says,
'you are there; if I descend into the pit of hell, you
are present.'* In both instances he acts mightily,

Ps 139:8

throwing down to earth and despoiling the cruel

*Jn 3:12

miser in the bottomless pit. It was only right that in ordering all things pleasingly, heavenly things* as well as earthly, he should establish all the others in peace by throwing down from aloft this trouble-maker. And, coming as he did to vanquish the jealous one in open combat here below, it was right that he should first give us the very necessary example of his own

*Eph 4:2

lowliness and meekness.* So, by the admirable arranging of Wisdom he appeared both gentle to his own and mighty to his enemies. What use indeed would it have been for the devil to be overcome by God if we had remained proud? It was necessary therefore for Mary to be engaged to Joseph: by this what was holy was kept secret from dogs, her virginity was attested to by her fiancé, the Virgin was spared all shame and her reputation was preserved. What could be wiser or more worthy of divine Providence? Only a plan like this could admit the witness of the heavenly mysteries and yet both keep the enemy at bay and preserve untainted the Virgin Mother's reputation. Could the just man have spared the adulteress? It is written indeed that 'her husband Joseph, being a just man, and unwilling to put her to

*Mt 1:19

shame, resolved to send her away quietly'.* Well enough, since he was a just man he was unwilling to put her the shame. He could never have been just had he consented, knowing her to be guilty. On the other hand he would not have been in the least just if he had condemned her when she was proven innocent. Because he was a just man and unwilling to put her to shame, he resolved to send her away quietly.

14. Why did he resolve to send her away? Once again listen to an opinion which is not only mine but comes from the Fathers. Joseph resolved to send her away for the same reason that Peter pushed the Lord away from him, saying 'Depart from me, for I

*Lk 5:8

am a sinful man, O Lord',* and for the same reason that the centurion prevented him from entering his house when he said, 'Lord, I am not worthy to have

*Mt 8:8

you come under my roof'.* It was the same with Joseph: he considered himself an unworthy sinful man and said to himself that he ought not to be living familiarly with so wonderful a person whose dignity awed him. He noticed that she was very obviously bearing the divine presence within her and it awed him. But not being able to penetrate this mystery, he resolved to send her away. Peter was afraid of the greatness of His power; the centurion feared the majesty of His presence. Joseph, like any other man, was seized with terror at the novelty of such a miracle, at the depths of this mystery. So he resolved to send her away quietly.

Why should you be surprised that Joseph considered himself unworthy to be the pregnant Virgin's consort? Remember that Elizabeth could not bear her presence without some fear and reverence. She said, 'And why is this granted to me, that the mother of my Lord should come to me?'* For this reason, too, Joseph resolved to send her away. But why should he do so 'quietly' and not openly?* Probably in order to avoid questions as to the cause of his divorce, to avoid having to give an explanation. What could this just man have answered to this stiff-necked people,* this unbelieving and rebellious people?* If he had said what he felt, that he could prove her purity, would the cruel and unbelieving Jews not have made rude gestures at him and stoned her? How could they possibly have believed in Truth lying silently in the womb when they were later to despise him as he cried out in the Temple?* What would they have done to him, as yet unmanifested, when they were to lay wicked hands upon him in the glistering flesh of his miracles? To avoid telling lies and exposing an innocent woman to public shame, he very rightly resolved to send her away quietly.

*Lk 1:43

*Lk 8:17

*Ex 32:9
*Rom 10:21

*Jn 7:28

15. Perhaps, however, there may be some who think that Joseph nurtured the same suspicion as would any other man and that, because of this suspicion, he—as a just man—did not wish to continue living with her, while on the other hand—as a kind man—not wanting to give her up as suspect, he resolved to send her away quietly. Let me reply briefly. Even if

this were the case, Joseph's doubt was necessary. It won for him the assurance of a divine confirmation. It is written: 'But as he considered this (that is, whether or not to send her away quietly) an angel appeared to him in a dream saying "Joseph, son of David, do not fear to take Mary as your wife, for that *Mt 1:20*   which is conceived of her is of the Holy Spirit" '.* All these are reasons why Mary was engaged to Joseph, or rather, as the Gospel puts it, 'to a man whose *Lk 1:27*   name was Joseph'.* He is called a man not because he was married to her, but because he was a man of courage. Or again, according to another Evangelist, he *Mt 1:19*   is not called simply a man, but 'her man'.* He was called what he must be thought to be. It was only right that he should be called her man, for it was necessary that he be thought so. In the same way he had the honor of being called the father of the Saviour even though he was not really so; as the same Evangelist says, 'Jesus was about thirty years of age, being the son (as was supposed) of Joseph'.* Yet he *Lk 3:23*   was neither the husband of the mother nor the father of the Son even though, as I have just shown, he was of necessity supposed to be both and was called so for the time being.

16. Imagine who this Joseph must have been and what sort of man he must have been to have deserved to be honored this way by God—in keeping with the divine plan, of course—that he was called and believed to be the father of God himself. Imagine his worth from his very name which, as you probably know, means 'increase'. And remember too that *Gen 37:8*   great patriarch who was sold once into Egypt.* Realize that the Joseph we are speaking of here not only shared that other great man's name, but also imitated his chastity, closely resembling him in innocence and grace. The first Joseph, sold by jealous brothers and led off to Egypt, prefigured the *Mt 26:14-16*   selling of Christ.* The second Joseph, fleeing jealous *Mt 2:13-14*   Herod,* carried Christ away into Egypt. The first, *2 Tim 4:7*   keeping faith* with the master, refused to couple *Gen 39:6-12*   with the mistress.* The second, recognizing that his

Lk 1:27

*Cf. Amadeus,
Hom. VIII*

Num 24:17

Pr 5:5

2 Cor 6:4

17. This verse ends: 'And the
Mary.'* Let us now say a few words
which means 'star of the sea' and is
the Virgin Mother.* Surely she is
likened to a star. The star sends forth it
harm to itself. In the same way the Vir
forth her son with no injury to herself. T
more diminishes the star's brightness than
Son his mother's integrity. She is indeed that
star risen out of Jacob* whose beam enlighten
earthly globe. She it is whose brightness both twin
in the highest heaven and pierces the pit of hel
and is shed upon earth, warming our hearts far more
than our bodies, fostering virtue and cauterizing
vice. She, I tell you, is that splendid and wondrous
star suspended as by necessity over this great wide
sea, radiant with merit and brilliant in example. O
you, whoever you are, who feel that in the tidal wave
of this world you are nearer to being tossed about
among the squalls and gales than treading on dry
land, if you do not want to founder in the tempest,
do not avert your eyes from the brightness of this
star. When the wind of temptation blows up within
you, when you strike upon the rock of tribulatior
gaze up at this star, call out to Mary. Whether you a
being tossed about by the waves of pride or ambi
or slander or jealousy, gaze up at this star, cal
to Mary. When rage or greed or fleshly desi
battering the skiff of your soul, gaze up a
When the immensity of your sins weighs y
and you are bewildered by the loathsomen
conscience, when the terrifying thought o
appalls you and you begin to founde
of sadness and despair, think of Mary
hardships,* in every doubt, think of
Mary. Keep her in your mouth,
heart. Follow the example of he
obtain the favor of her prayer.
will never go astray. Asking her h
despair. Keeping her in your though
wander away. With your hand in
never stumble. With her protecting you

...he mother of the Lord, was a virgin, watched
...er in faithful continence. The first had the gift
...terpreting the hidden secrets of dreams. The
...d not only knew of heavenly mysteries but
... participated in them. The first Joseph stored up
...n for himself and for all the people; the second
...s given charge of the bread come down from
...aven* for his sake and for that of the whole   *Jn 6:41*
...orld. There can be no doubt that this Joseph, to
whom the mother of the Saviour was engaged, was a
good and faithful man.* I tell you, he was the wise   *Mt 25:21*
and faithful servant whom his Lord set to be the
comfort of his mother and the bread-winner for his
body. He was God's only and most faithful coadjutor
in his great plan on earth. It is also said in this context that Joseph was of the house of David.* Cer-   *Lk 1:27*
tainly he was of the house of David! This Joseph was
a man of truly royal lineage, noble of race and still
more noble of mind. He is a real son of David, not
unworthy of his father David. The son of David not
only by blood, but by faith, I say, by holiness, by
devotedness. He was one whom the Lord found to be
another David, a man after his heart,* one to whom   *Acts 13:22*
he had committed the most secret and the most
sacred of all the holy mysteries of his heart. God
made known to him, as to another David, the uncertain and hidden* things of his wisdom. God granted   *Ps 51:6*
...hat he should not be ignorant of the mystery which
...o prince of this world had any notion of. To him it
...s given not only to see and to hear what many
...gs and prophets had longed to see* and did not   *Mt 13:17*
...to hear and did not hear, but even to carry him,
...ke him by the hand, to hug and kiss him, to feed
...nd to keep him safe.

...t only Joseph, but Mary as well, we must sup-
...descended from the house of David. She would
...ve been engaged to a man of the house of
...f sh... herself had not also been of this royal
...e truth which the Lord swore to David
...hed in her. He was the only trustee and
...he fulfilment of the promise.

be afraid. With her leading you, you will never tire.
Her kindness will see you through to the end. Then
you will know by your own experience how true it
is that 'the Virgin's name was Mary'.*   *Lk 1:27*

But now we must rest awhile for fear that we do
no more than cast a fleeting glance at the brightness
of such splendid light. And if I may appropriate the
words of the Apostle: 'It is good that we are here'*   *Mk 17:4*
sweetly to contemplate in silence what no long-
winded discourse could ever adequately explain. By
devout contemplation of this twinkling star, this
interval will allow us to refresh our minds for the
discourse that follows.

HOMILY III

WHENEVER I see that the words of Holy Scripture suit my purpose I willingly make them my own so that what I have to say may charm my readers at least by the beauty of the vessels. That is why, for example, I now begin with this prophetic utterance, 'Woe is me'. Not because I have held my tongue as the prophet did, but because I dare to speak, 'for I am a man of unclean lips'.* Alas! I cannot forget how many vain, lying and dirty words I once vomited out of this foul mouth from which I now presume to speak about heavenly things. I am very much afraid that I shall hear said to me, 'What right have you to recite my statutes or to take my covenant on your lips?'* Oh, if only someone would bring down to me from the altar on high not just one burning coal* but a huge fiery globe by which the ingrained and thick rust would be entirely burnt out of my lewd mouth. Perhaps then I should be worthy to repeat in my own very ordinary language those gracious and chaste words of the angel to the Virgin and of the Virgin to him.

*Is 6:5

*Ps 50:16

*Is 6:6

The Evangelist says: 'And the angel went into her—to Mary of course—and said, "Hail, full of grace, the Lord is with you".'* 'Went in' where? Into the private chamber of her modest room where, I suppose, having shut the door she was praying to the Father in secret.* Angels are accustomed to taking their stand beside those who pray, and they delight in those whom they see lifting pure hands in prayer.* They are happy to be able to carry to God in the fragrance of its sweetness the sacrifices of holy

*Lk 1:26

*Mt 6:6

*1 Tim 2:8

*Eph 5:2

*Sir 35:8

*Ezek 1:12

devotion.* By going into Mary and greeting her so reverently the Angel showed just how pleasing were her prayers to the Most High.* It was not hard for the angel to enter the Virgin's private room through a closed door; it was natural to him, for so great was the subtleness of his nature that an iron gate could not have prevented him from going wherever his mission sent him.* Angelic spirits are not hindered by walls. All visible things give way to them and every bulky mass, however thick and solid, is penetrable and pervious to them. There is no reason to suspect that the angel found the Virgin's little door ajar. She clearly had it in mind to flee human company, to avoid conversation lest the silence of one given to prayer should be disturbed and the purity of one given to chastity be assailed. Surely then the most prudent virgin had at that time closed the door of her private room to men, but not to angels. Thus, even though the angel could go into her the way was barred to any human being.

*Lk 1:28
*Acts 6:8
*Acts 2:4

*Col 2:9

2. 'The Angel came in to her and said, "Hail, full of grace, the Lord is with you".'* In the Acts of the Apostles we read that Stephen was full of grace* and that the Apostles were filled with the Holy Spirit,* but quite differently from Mary. The fullness of the godhead did not dwell bodily* in Stephen as it did in Mary. The Apostles did not conceive by the Holy Spirit as she did. 'Hail, full of grace, the Lord is with you', said the angel. What wonder is there that she would be full of grace when the Lord was with her? But what is more astonishing is that when the angel arrived he found the person by whom he had been sent was already with the Virgin. Could God have hastened down to earth more swiftly than his winging messenger in order to get to earth before him? I should not be surprised. While the King was on his couch, the Virgin's nard was sending forth its fragrance* and a sweet smelling smoke was rising up in the sight of his glory, and in this way she found grace in the Lord's eyes.* Those who were gathered round him exclaimed, 'who is this coming up from

*Sg 1:11

*Lk 1:30

the wilderness, like a column of smoke, perfumed with myrrh and frankincense?'* At once the King set out from his holy place.* He rejoiced like a giant to run his course.* And though he set out from the highest heaven, he was moved by so great a desire that he sped ahead of his messenger and came to the Virgin whom he loved, whom he had chosen for his own, whose beauty he ardently desired.* It is this same lover whom the Church, looking from afar and seeing him coming,* greets with joy and gladness exclaiming, 'Behold, he comes leaping upon the mountains, bounding over the hills'.*

*Sg 3:6
*Is 26:21
*Ps 19:5

*Ps 45:11

*Jn 1:9

*Sg 2:8

3. The king rightly desired the Virgin's beauty. She was doing what her father David long before had advised her to do when he said, 'Harken, O daughter, consider and incline your ear, forget your people and your father's house and the King will desire your beauty'.* She had both heard and seen, not like those who, hearing do not listen* and seeing do not understand.* When she heard she believed,† when she saw she understood. She inclined her ear, that is, to obedience and her heart to discipline. And she forgot her own people and her father's house. She was not anxious to increase her people by giving birth to a new generation, she did not seek to leave an heir to her father's house. Whatever honor she might have had from her father's house was all counted as refuse that she might gain Christ.* Nor was she disappointed in any way. She was able to claim a son in Christ and yet not violate her vow of chastity. Truly may we say that she was full of grace: while retaining the grace of virginity she was blessed in addition with the honor of motherhood.

*Ps 45:10
*Mk 4:12
*cf. Wis 4:14
†cf. Jn 5:24

*Phil 3:8

4. 'Hail full of grace, the Lord is with you', he said. He did not say, 'The Lord is in you' but 'the Lord is with you'. For God, simple by nature, is equally and entirely everywhere at once. But in his rational creatures he is present in a different way than in other creatures. Again, even among his rational creatures, he is not present with the same efficacy

in the bad as in the good. Though he is present in irrational creatures, they cannot be said to grasp him. And though every rational creature can grasp him by some concept [of him], it is only the good who can grasp him by love as well. Only the good, because of the union of their will with his, deserve to have it said of them that he is with them. That they will what he wills does not demean God because they have bent their wills to his justice: there is no conflict and they are spiritually united to their God. But if this may be said of all the saints, it is especially true of Mary. Her will was in such great harmony with God's that he joined not only her will, but even her flesh, to himself so completely that from his substance and the Virgin's He made one Christ, or rather He became one Christ. He was neither entirely from God nor entirely from the Virgin, yet he was fully God's son and also fully the Virgin's son. Nor were there two sons, but the one son of them both. Therefore the angel said 'Hail full of grace, the Lord is with you'. Not only the Lord, your son, is with you, whom you have clothed with your flesh, but also the Lord, the Holy Spirit by whom you conceived. The Father is with you, I say, he who makes his Son yours. The Son is with you, he who in order to bring about within you a marvellous mystery shut himself in a marvellous way in the retirement of your womb and preserved the seal of your virginity. The Holy Spirit is with you, he who being one with the Father and the Son, sanctifies your womb. Indeed 'the Lord is with you'!

*Lk 1:28

5. 'Blessed are you among women.'* To these words of Elizabeth we must add those which she spoke immediately afterwards: 'And blessed is the fruit of

*Lk 1:42

your womb.'* It is not because you are blessed that the fruit is blessed as well, but you are blessed because he has come to you with the blessings of

*Ps 21:3

sweetness.* The fruit of your womb is truly blessed,

*Gal 3:8

for in him all nations shall be blessed* and of his

*Jn 1:16

fullness you also have received,* as have we all, yet how differently. Therefore you are blessed, blessed

among women, though he was not blessed among
men or even among the angels. As the Apostle says,
he is 'God above all, blessed for ever'.* We are   *Rom 9:5*
accustomed to speaking of a blessed man, blessed
bread, a blessed woman, the blessed earth and to
remark on any other creature which we know has
received a blessing, but in quite a special way is the
fruit of your womb blessed because he is God above
all, blessed for ever.

6. Blessed then is the fruit of your womb.* Blessed   *Lk 1:42*
in his fragrance, blessed in his savor, blessed in his
comeliness. It was the fragrance of this sweet smelling
fruit that [Isaac] smelt when he said, 'This is the
fragrance of my son, similar to the smell of a field
which the Lord has blessed'.* Ah! Is he not truly   *Gen 27:27*
blessed whom the Lord has blessed? And someone
else, having tasted the savor of this fruit, gave vent
to his satisfaction saying, 'Taste and see how sweet
the Lord is'.* And in another place, 'How great is   *Ps 34:8*
the abundance of your sweetness, Lord, which you
have laid up for those who fear you.'* And someone   *Ps 31:19*
else said, 'If only you could taste and see how sweet
the Lord is'.* And the Fruit himself, inviting us to go   *1 Pet 2:3*
to him, said of himself, 'Those who eat me will
hunger for more, and those who drink me will thirst
for more'.* He was referring to the sweetness of his   *Sir 24:29*
savor* which, once it has been tasted, whets the   *Wis 16:20*
appetite for more. This good fruit* is both food and   *Mt 3:10, 7:19*
drink to the souls of those who hunger and thirst for
righteousness.*   *Mt 5:6*

You have heard of his fragrance; you have heard of
his savor. Now listen about his comeliness. If it is true,
as Scripture says,* that the fruit of death was not   *Gen 3:3*
only sweet to eat, but also beautiful to look at, how
much greater must be the life-giving beauty of this
living fruit upon which, according to another passage
of Scripture, 'even the angels longed to look'?* He   *1 Pet 1:12*
who said 'Out of Sion comes the loveliness of his
beauty'* was contemplating in his mind this comeli-   *Ps 50:2*
ness and desired ardently to see it also in the flesh.
And, in case you think he was praising some

ordinary beauty, recall that you read in another
psalm, 'You are the comeliest of the sons of men:
grace is poured upon your lips. Therefore God has
Ps 45:3   blessed you for ever'.

Lk 1:42   7. Blessed, then, is the fruit of your womb, whom
Ps 45:3   God has blessed for ever. And in virtue of this
Lk 1:42   blessing you too are blessed among women, for a
Mt 7:18   bad tree cannot bear good fruit. Blessed, I say,
among women, you are free not only from the
general curse which decrees that 'In pain you shall
Gen 3:16   bring forth children', but because you escape no
less that other curse uttered long afterwards: cursed
Ex 23:26   be the childless woman in Israel. Yours was an
exceptional blessing. You were not childless, yet you
did not bring forth your child in pain. This is the
Sir 40:1   hard burden and the heavy yoke laid on every
daughter of Eve. If they bear children, they are in
anguish; if they are childless, then they are cursed.
The pain keeps them from having children and the
curse from not having them. What will you do, virgin
maid, you who have heard these words and read
them? Will you give birth to a child and suffer agony
or remain sterile and be cursed? Which will you
Mt 25:2   choose, wise virgin? 'On every side,' she says, 'I am
Dan 13:22   hemmed in, yet I prefer to be cursed and to remain
chaste than to conceive a child because of lust and
then to bring him forth in pain deservedly. On one
side I see a curse but no sin, and on the other, not
only sin but anguish as well. Yet what is this curse
but men's censure? There is no real reason why a
childless woman should be cursed except because she
is considered shameful and contemptible as if she
were barren and worthless, and this is only so in
1 Cor 4:3   Israel. But for me it is a very small thing that I
should be displeasing to men when I can present
2 Cor 11:2   myself a pure virgin to Christ.' O wise virgin! O
dedicated virgin! Whoever taught you that virginity is
pleasing to God? What law, what justice, what page of
the Old Testament either commands or counsels or
urges you to live in the flesh yet not according to the
cf. Rom 8:4   flesh, to live on earth an angelic life? Where did you

read, blessed Virgin, that 'wisdom according to the
flesh is death'* and to 'make no provision for the *Rom 8:6*
flesh never gratifying its desire'?* Where did you read *Rom 13:14*
that virgins will sing a new song which no other
person can sing?* That they 'follow the Lamb *Rev 14:3*
wherever he goes'?* Where did you read that those *Rev 14:4*
who make themselves eunuchs for the sake of the
kingdom of heaven* are praised? Where did you read; *Mt 19:12*
though living in the flesh, we do not war with the
flesh's weapons?* Or: he who gives his virgin daugh- *2 Cor 10:3*
ter in marriage does well, but that he who does not
give her in marriage does better still?* Where did you *1 Cor 7:38*
hear: 'I wish that all were as I am myself,'* and, 'It *1 Cor 7:7*
is good for a man if he follows my advice'?* *1 Cor 7:40*
'Concerning virgins I have no command', he says,
'but I give my advice'?* In your case, however, I *1 Cor 7:26*
would say there is no other command, advice or
example, but the anointing which taught you about
everything,* the living and active Word of God.† He *1 Jn 2:27*
was your Master long before he became your son. He †*Heb 4:12*
instructed your mind before he clothed himself with
your flesh. It was thus you resolved to present
yourself to Christ as a virgin* before you knew that *2 Cor 11:2*
you would also be presented to him as his mother.
You chose to be despised in Israel. You preferred to
risk being cursed for barrenness in order to be found
pleasing to him who searched you out. Lo, this curse
is changed into a blessing: your barrenness is rewarded
with child bearing.

8. Virgin maid, open up your bosom, enlarge your
womb, for he who is mighty is about to do great
things for you.* According to the Law in Israel you *Lk 1:49*
are cursed, but henceforth all generations will call
you blessed.* Do not distrust your own childbearing, *Lk 1:48*
wise Virgin, it will not stain your integrity. You shall
conceive, but without sin. You will be heavy with
child and yet not bowed down. You will give birth,
but not in sadness.* Though you know no man you *Gen 3:6*
will bear a son. What sort of son? You are to become
the mother of a child whose father is God himself. A
son of the brightness of the Father will be the

crown of your love. The wisdom of the Father's heart shall become the fruit of your virginal womb. You are to give birth to God, you conceive by God. Take courage, pregnant Virgin, chaste maid with child, undefiled mother, for you will no longer be cursed in Israel or considered barren. And if Israel still curses you in fleshly terms, not because you are barren but because they are jealous of your child-bearing, then remember that Christ also will bear the curse of the cross and it is he who blesses you, his mother, in heaven. But you are blessed on earth as well by the angel and by all generations after you. So 'blessed are you among women, and blessed is the fruit of your womb'.*

Lk 1:42

9. 'But when she heard this, she was troubled at the saying and pondered what sort of greeting this might be.'* It is usual for virgins—those who really are virgins—always to be timid and never to feel safe. They are so constantly on guard against danger that they easily take fright, because they know that they carry a precious treasure in an earthen vessel* and that it is very difficult to live as an angel among men, to follow the ways of heaven on earth and to lead a heavenly life while still in the flesh. Any new or unexpected thing they suspect of being harmful and they think they see snares everywhere. That explains why Mary was troubled by what the angel said to her. She was troubled, but not distressed. It is written, 'I am troubled and do not speak, but I consider the days of old, I remember the years long past'.* And so it was with Mary. She was troubled, she did not speak, but she pondered what sort of greeting this might be.* That she should be troubled is only virginal reserve. Not to be distressed shows courage. That she was silent and pondered shows prudence. But she pondered what sort of greeting this might be. This wise Virgin knew only too well that Satan's angel often disguises himself as an angel of light* and because she was all humility and simplicity she had never hoped to hear such words coming from a holy angel. That was why she pondered what sort of

Lk 1:29

2 Cor 4:7

Ps 77:4-5

Lk 1:29

2 Cor 11:14, 12:7

greeting this might be.

10. Then the angel, looking at the Virgin, immediately realized that she was turning over in her mind
varied thoughts, and allayed her fears, cleared away
her doubtfulness. He called her familiarly by her
name, gently comforted her with soothing words
saying, 'Do not be afraid, Mary, you have found favor
with God'.* It is as if he wanted to say, There is no   *Lk 1:30*
ruse here, no trickery. You need not suspect any
harm, or any trap. I am not a man, but a spirit, an
angel of God not of Satan. Do not be afraid, Mary,
you have found favor with God. Oh, if you only
knew how pleasing your humility is to the Most High
and what greatness has been prepared for you close
to himself, you would not consider yourself too
unworthy of this greeting and this homage. Why
should you not find favor with angels when you have
found favor with God? You have found what you
were seeking,* you have found what no one before   *Mt 7:7*
you has ever been able to find, you have found favor
with God. What is this favor? Peace between God and
men, the destruction of death, the restoration of life.
This is the favor you have found with God. And this
will be a sign for you:* behold you will conceive and   *Lk 2:12*
bear a son, and you shall call his name Jesus.'*   *Lk 1:31*

Wise Virgin, understand by the name of this
promised son what great and special favor you have
found with God. 'And you shall call his name Jesus',
said the angel. Another Evangelist gives the reason
for this name. He records the interpretation given by
the angel: 'he will save his people for their sins'.*   *Mt 1:21*

11. I have read of two Jesuses who prefigured the
one we are dealing with here. Both were leaders of
their nations. One of them led his people out of
Babylon and the other took them into the promised
land. Both defended the people against the enemy,
but did they save them from their sins? Yet this Jesus,
our Jesus, not only saves his people from their sins,   *Ps 116:9,*
he leads them into the land of the living.* It is he   *27:13*
who will save his people from their sins.* Who is this   *Mt 1:21*

*Lk 7:49
*cf. Lk 18:13

*Ps 33:12

*Mt 15:8

*Lk 6:46

*Lk 24:44
*1 Cor 6:4

*1 Pet 2:18
*Mt 11:29

*Ps 33:12

*Is 19:25
*Jn 1:15

*Ps 18:43-4

*Lk 1:32

*Ps 145:3
†Ps 113:5

who even forgives sins?* Ah, if only the Lord Jesus would deign to count me, a sinner,* among his people that he might save me from my sins. How blessed is the people whose God is the Lord* Jesus, for he will save his people from their sins. I am afraid that a good many say they belong to his people whom he himself does not count as his people. I am afraid that to many of those who appear to be the most religious among his people he will one day say, 'This people honors me with their lips, but their heart is far from me.'* The Lord Jesus knows his own. He knows them and he has chosen them from the beginning. Does he not say, 'Why do you call me "Lord, Lord", and do not do what I tell you?'* Do you want to know whether or not you belong to his people? Or rather, do you want to be among his people? Do what Jesus says, and he will count you among his people. Do what the Lord Jesus commands in the Gospel, what he commands in the Law and the prophets;* what he commands by his ministers who are in the Church.* Be subject to his vicars, your leaders, not only to those who are modest and gentle, but also to the overbearing,* and learn from Jesus himself that he is meek and humble of heart,* then you will be numbered among that blessed people of his whom he has chosen as his heritage,* you will be one of the praiseworthy people whom the Lord blessed when he said, 'You are the work of my hands, Israel my heritage'.* And for fear that you should strive to imitate the carnal Israel, he bears witness* saying, 'A people whom I have not known have served me, as soon as they heard of me they obeyed me'.*

12. Let us now hear what this same Angel thinks about this child to whom, even before his conception, he has given so great a name. He says, 'He will be great and will be called the Son of the Most High'.* Is he not great when there is no end of his greatness?* And he says, 'Who is great like our God?'† He is clearly great, he is as great as the Most High, for he is himself none other than the Most High. Nor, being

the Son of the Most High, did he count it robbery to be equal to the Most High.* The one who must be thought to have premeditated robbery is he who, having been called out of nothing into the form of an angel, likened himself to his Maker and snatched at what belongs to the Son of the Most High, to him who in the form of God was not made by God but begotten. The Most High Father, although he is almighty, could neither fashion a creature equal to himself nor beget a Son unequal to himself. He made the angel very great then, but not as great as himself, and therefore not most high. That the only-begotten Son whom he did not make but begot, the Almighty from the Almighty, the Most High from the Most High, coeternal with the eternal, claimed to be compared to him in every way, he thought neither robbery nor affrontery. How rightly then will he be called great: he is the Son of the Most High.

*Phil 2:6

13. But why does the angel say 'He will be' and not 'he is' great? His greatness, forever unvarying, is not subject to growth. He will not be greater after his conception than before. Is it possible the angel meant to say that he who is a great God will become a great man? In that case he was right to say 'He will be great', for he will be a great man, a great teacher, a great prophet. We do in fact read in the Gospel of him, 'A great prophet has risen up among us'.* In the past there were lesser prophets who foretold the coming of this great prophet: 'Behold, a great prophet shall come and he shall restore Jerusalem.'* You, however, virgin maid, will give birth to a little child, you will feed a little child and suckle a little one. But as you gaze at this little one, think how great he is. He will indeed be great, for God will magnify him in the sight of kings* and all kings will come to adore him, all nations shall serve him.* So let your soul magnify the Lord,* for he will be great and will be called the Son of the Most High. He will be great and he who is mighty will do great things in you, holy is his name.* What holier name could he have than to be called the son of the Most

*Lk 7:16

*Advent I Antiphon at None.

*Sir 45:3
*Ps 72:11
*Lk 1:46

*Lk 1:49

High? May this great Lord be magnified by us little
ones as well; that he might make us great, he was
made a little child. 'Unto us a child is born,' someone

*Is 9:6
said, 'For us a son is given.'* For us, I repeat, not for
himself. He who was born of the Father before all ages
was of more noble birth and had no need to be born
in time from a mother. And he was not even born for
the angels. They had him great among them and
had no need of a little child. He was born for us,
therefore, and given to us because we need him.

14. Now that he has been born and given to us, let
us accomplish the purpose of this birth and this
donation. He came for our good, let us use him to
*Phil 2:12
our good, let us work out our salvation* from the
*Mt 18:2
Saviour. Look, a little child is put in our midst.* O
little child so desired by your children! You are
*1 Cor 14:20
indeed a little child, but a child in evil-doing,* not a
child in wisdom. Let us make every effort to become
*Mt 18:3
like this little child.* Because he is meek and humble
*Mt 11:29
in heart,* let us learn from him, lest he who is great,
even God, should have been made a little man for
*Gal 2:21
nothing, lest he should have died to no purpose,*
and have been crucified in vain. Let us learn his
humility, imitate his gentleness, embrace his love,
*1 Pet 4:13
†Rev 1:5
share his sufferings,* be washed in his blood.† Let us
*1 Jn 2:2
offer him the propitiation for our sins* because for
this he was born and given for us. Let us offer him up
*Jn 1:11
in the sight of the Father, offer him too to his own,*
for the Father did not spare his own Son but gave
*Rom 8:31
him up for us all.* And the Son emptied himself,
*Phil 2:7
taking the form of a servant.* He freely poured out
his soul in death and was numbered with brigands and
he bore the sins of many and interceded for trans-
*Is 53:12
gressors* that they might not perish. How can they
perish whom the Son prayed might not perish, and
*Jn 10:10
for whose life the Father gave up his Son to death?*
We equally may hope therefore for forgiveness from
them both for they are equally merciful in their
steadfast love, united in a single powerful will, one in
the substance of the Godhead, in which together
with the Holy Spirit, they live and reign, one God
for ever and ever. Amen.

HOMILY IV

THERE IS no doubt that whatever we say in praise of the mother touches the Son, and when we honor the Son we detract nothing from the mother's glory. For if, as Solomon says, 'A wise son is the glory of his father',* how much more glorious is it to become the mother of Wisdom himself? But how can I attempt to praise her whom the prophets have proclaimed, the angel has acknowledged and the evangelist has described as praiseworthy? I will not praise her then. I do not dare to. I will only mull over devoutly what the Holy Spirit has already said by the mouth of the Evangelist. *Pr 13:1

He goes on to say, 'And the Lord will give to him the throne of his father David'.* Those are the very words spoken by the angel to the Virgin about the Son who had been promised to her, and by them he promised also that He should possess the kingship of David. No one doubts that the Lord Jesus belongs to David's lineage. But I wonder how God will give him the throne of his father David when he never reigned in Jerusalem,* still more, he refused to comply with the wishes of the crowd when they wanted to make him king,* and he protested before Pilate that 'My kingship is not of this world'.* Moreover, is it such a great thing to promise that he who sits enthroned upon the cherubim* and whom the prophet saw sitting upon a throne high and lifted up* will sit upon the throne of his father David? However, as we know, there is another Jerusalem meant, one different from that which now is,* where David reigned, one far more noble and far richer. I think that this is the one *Lk 1:32

*Jer 13:13

*Jn 6:15
*Jn 18:36

*Ps 99:1
*Is 6:1

*Gal 4:25

meant here, in the manner of speaking frequently
found in Scripture, where the sign means the thing
signified. So, God gave him the throne of his father
David when he set him up as king on Sion, his holy
Ps 2:6   hill. The prophet shows clearly which kingdom he is
speaking about when he says that God set him up
'on Sion' and not 'in Sion'. That is probably what he
meant when he used the word *on*, because David
reigned *in* Sion whereas to reign *on* Sion is the royal
prerogative of the person of whom it was said to
David, 'Of the fruit of your body will I set on your
Ps 132:11   throne' and of whom by another prophet it was
said: 'He will sit on the throne of David, and [lay
Is 9:7   claim] on his kingdom'. Do you see, everywhere
you find the word *on*? On Sion, on the throne, on
the kingdom. 'The Lord will give him the throne of
his father David,' not the symbolic, temporal, earthly
throne, but the real, eternal, heavenly one. If it is
called David's, this is because, as we have already
said, the throne on which he sat in time bore the
image of the eternal throne.

2. 'And he shall reign over the house of Jacob for
Lk 1:32-33   ever; and of his kingdom there shall be no end.'
Here again, if we interpret this as the temporal house
of Jacob, how could he reign eternally over a house
which is not eternal? We shall have to find an eternal
house of Jacob over which he, whose kingdom will
have no end, may reign eternally. When Pilate asked
'Shall I crucify your king?' did the frenzied house of
Jacob not wickedly deny him and stupidly reject
him, screaming back their answer as with one voice;
Jn 19:15   'We have no king but Caesar'? Consult the Apostle,
then, and he will help you discern the one who is a
Jew in secret from one who is so only in public, the
Rom 2:28   circumcision in the Spirit from that of the flesh, the
spiritual Israel from the fleshly, the sons of Abra-
Rom 9:8   ham's faith from the children of his flesh. For, as he
himself tells us, 'not all who are descended from
Israel belong to Israel, and not all are children of
Rom 9:6   Abraham because they are his seed'. Draw your
conclusions then and say, 'Similarly, not all who

are born of Jacob are to be counted among Jacob's
household,' for Jacob is Israel.* Consequently only   *Heb 11:21*
those who are perfect in Jacob's faith may be
numbered in the house of Jacob, or rather, it is
only they who belong to that spiritual and eternal
house of Jacob over which the Lord Jesus will reign
eternally. Who is there among us who, in keeping
with the etymology of the name Jacob, supplants*   *Gen 27:36*
the devil from his heart† and struggles* with his vices   †Lk 8:12
and evil desires to prevent sin from holding sway in   *Gen 32:24*
the body of his death* and to let Jesus reign there   *Gal 5:24*
now by his grace and for eternity by his glory?
Blessed are they in whom Jesus 'will reign eternally',* for they will reign with him and of his   *Lk 1:33*
kingdom there will be no end.* Oh, how glorious is   *Rev 20:6*
that kingdom where kings have assembled, have come
together* to praise and glorify him who is above all,† *Ps 48:5*
King of kings and Lord of lords,* in the brilliant   †Eph 4:6
contemplation of whom the righteous shine as the   *1 Tim 6:15*
sun* in the kingdom of their Father. Oh, if only   *Mt 13:43*
Jesus would remember me, a sinner, when he shows
favor to his people,* when he comes into his   *Ps 106:4*
kingdom.* Oh, if on that day when he delivers his   *Lk 23:42*
kingdom to God the Father* he would but deign to   *1 Cor 15:24*
visit me in his salvation that I might be admitted to
the prosperity of his chosen ones and rejoice in the
gladness of his nation, that even I might praise him
with his heritage.* Come, meanwhile, Lord Jesus,†   *Ps 106:4-5*
thrust out all causes of sin* from your kingdom, my   †Rev 22:20
soul, that you may reign there as you should. Avarice   *Mt 18:41*
comes and claims a throne within me; vainglory
craves to hold sway in me; pride wants to lord it over
me. Sensuality cries, 'I will rule';* ambition and   *1 Kings 1:5*
detraction, envy and anger fight over me within me.
Yet I, as far as I can, put up a fight. I push them back
with all my might. I call out to my Lord Jesus. I
defend myself for his sake, for I know that I am his
by right. I hold him as my God, I hold him as my
Lord, and I declare, 'I have no other king than
Jesus'.* Come then, Lord, scatter them by your   *Jn 19:15*
power,* and you shall reign over me, for you are my   *Ps 59:11*
king and my God who order deliverance for Jacob.*   *Ps 44:4*

3. 'But Mary said to the angel, "How can this be,
since I know no man?" '* At first, as long as she was
doubtful, she prudently kept silence and pondered
what sort of greeting this might be,* preferring, of
course, humbly to give no reply rather than to speak
hastily about matters of which she knew nothing.
But once she was reassured, after having thought
things out carefully (for though the angel was speaking to her from without, God was inwardly persuading
her—for the Lord was with her as the angel had said,
'the Lord is with you'*) once she was strengthened
by the faith which castes out fear,* and by the joy
which casts out confusion, she said to the angel, 'How
can this be, since I know no man?' She does not
doubt the event, but wonders how it shall occur. She
is not asking *whether* it will happen, but *how*. It is as
if she said, 'Since my Lord, who is the witness of my
conscience* knows that his servant has vowed not to
know a man, by what dispensation and in what way
might it please him that this should happen? If I have
to break my vow in order to bear this son, I should
both rejoice about the son and be sorry about my
vow. Yet let his will be done. But if I conceive as a
virgin, if I give birth as a virgin, neither of which is
impossible if he shall please,* then I shall know for
sure* that he has regarded the low estate of his
handmaiden.'* 'How (then) can this be, since I know
no man?' 'And the Angel said to her, "The Holy
Spirit will come upon you, and the power of the
Most High will overshadow you." '* Further up she
was said to be 'full of grace'.* How then can it now
be said, 'The Holy Spirit will come upon you and
the power of the Most High will overshadow you'?
Could she have been full of grace when she had not
yet received the Holy Spirit, who is the giver of all
grace? But if the Holy Spirit was already within her,
how can he be promised anew as though he were
about to visit her again? Was that perhaps why he
did not simply say, 'he will come in you', but 'upon
you', because whereas he was already within her by
abundant grace, he is said to come upon her on account of the fullness* of the even more abundant

*Lk 1:34

*Lk 1:29

*Lk 1:28
*1 Jn 4:18

*2 Cor 1:12

*Lk 1:37
*Acts 12:11
*Lk 1:48

*Lk 1:34
*Lk 1:28

*2 Cor 4:15

grace which was to be poured out upon her? And yet, when she was already full of grace, how could she receive more? And if she could receive something more, how was it possible to say before that she was already full of grace? Could it be that the first grace had filled only her soul, and that the second was now to be showered in her womb because the fullness of divinity which already dwelt within her spiritually, as it does in many a saint, will now begin to dwell within her corporally* as it had done in no other saint?

*Col 2:9

4. He said then, 'The Holy Spirit will come upon you, and the power of the Most High will overshadow you.'* What does 'and the power of the Most High will overshadow you' mean? 'Let him who can grasp this.'* Who indeed can, except perhaps she who alone deserved to have this most blessed experience, who can grasp by his intelligence and discern with his reason not only the way in which the inaccessible splendor could pour itself out into a virginal womb but also how, in order that she might support the approach of the inaccessible, it became a shade for the rest of this body, a small portion of which he had vivified and appropriated? And perhaps it was for this reason the angel used the words 'he will overshadow you', because the event was so great a mystery that the Trinity wished to accomplish it in the Virgin alone and with her alone, and she alone was allowed to understand* it because she alone was allowed to experience it. Let us admit then that 'The Holy Spirit will come upon you' means 'you will become pregnant by his power'. And the words, 'The power of the Most High shall overshadow you', mean 'the means by which you are to conceive by the Holy Spirit is that the power of God and the wisdom of God,* Christ, will be so concealed and so hidden in the shadowing of his most secret counsel that it shall be known only to him and to you.' It is as if the angel replied to the Virgin, 'Why ask me about something which you are going soon to experience in yourself? You will find out, you will find out, how happily you

*Lk 1:35

*Mt 19:12

*Mt 13:11

*1 Cor 1:24

will find out, and your teacher will be none other than he who works this [within you]. I have been sent only to announce this virginal conception, not to bring it about. This is something which can only be taught by the giver, and learnt only by the receiver. "Therefore the Holy to be born of you will be called the Son of God." '* This means: You are to conceive, but by the Holy Spirit, not by man. You will therefore conceive the power of the Most High, the Son of God. 'Therefore the Holy to be born of you will be called the Son of God.' This means: He who comes from the bosom of the Father* into your womb will not only overshadow you, he will even take to himself something of your substance. He who is already the Son of God begotten of the Father before all ages will henceforth be acknowledged to be your son as well. In this way, the son born of God will be yours, and the child born of you will be God's, in such a way that there be not two sons, however, but only one. And although he has one [nature] of you and another of God, yet you will not each have your own son, but he will be the one Son of you both'.

*Lk 1:35

*Jn 1:18

5. 'And therefore the Holy to be born of you will be called the Son of God.' Please notice how reverently he says 'The Holy to be born of you'. Why does he say simply the 'Holy' and nothing else? I think that it must have been because there was no name by which he could correctly or worthily qualify that extraordinary, that magnificent, that awesome being who was going to unite the Virgin's most chaste flesh to his own soul in the only begotten Son of the Father. Had he said the 'holy flesh' or the 'holy man' or 'the holy child', whatever he might have found to say would have seemed to him inadequate. So he uttered the indefinite 'Holy', because whatever it was the Virgin bore was without any doubt holy, and uniquely holy, both sanctified by the Spirit* and assumed by the Word.

*1 Pet 1:2

6. The angel went on to say, 'And behold, your

kinswoman Elizabeth in her old age has also con-
ceived a son'.* Why was it necessary to inform the   *Lk 1:36*
Virgin that a barren woman had conceived? Did he
perhaps wish to strengthen her by this latest miracle
because she was still doubtful and incredulous of his
words? Certainly not. We read that this same angel
punished Zechariah's doubt,* but we never read that   *Lk 1:18-20*
Mary was blamed for anything. On the contrary, we
know that her faith was praised by Elizabeth in prophetic words, 'Blessed are you who believed that
there would be a fulfilment of what was spoken to
you from the Lord'.* Mary was told of the concep-   *Lk 1:45*
tion of her barren kinswoman so that, one miracle
following upon another, joy should be added to joy.
What is more, as she was on the point of conceiving
the Son of the Father's love* in the joy of the Holy   *Col 1:13*
Spirit, she needed to be inflamed by a great fire of
love and gladness. For only in the most dedicated
and happiest of hearts could such a flood of sweetness and happiness be welcomed. Or it may have
been that Mary was told of Elizabeth's conception
because it was only fitting she should learn news
which was soon going to be spread everywhere from
the Angel rather than from a human being, lest it
should seem that the Mother of God was kept
distant from her Son's plans if she were ignorant
of what was going on in the world around her. Or it
may be that Mary was told of the conception of
Elizabeth so that, having been informed of the
arrival of both the Saviour and his precursor and
knowing the exact date and sequence of events, she
would later be better able to give a true account to
the writers and preachers of the Gospel, having been
fully informed about all these heavenly mysteries
from the beginning. Or the fact that Elizabeth had
conceived may have been told to Mary so that, hearing that her cousin already advancing in years was
with child, this young girl might be mindful of her
duty and hasten to visit her,* thus giving opportunity   *Lk 1:39*
to the little prophet to offer the first fruits of his
office to his still smaller Lord. And while the mothers
ran to greet each other, affection was roused in the

babes from womb to womb, thus the first miracle was the occasion of a second, more wonderful one.

7. Be careful not to hope that the great things announced by the angel were to be brought about by him, however. If you wish to know by whom they will be accomplished, listen to the angel say, 'For with God no word will be impossible'.* It is as if he would say, 'These things which I now faithfully promise will come about not by my power, but by his who sent me, for with him no word is impossible'. Indeed, how could any word be impossible to him when he made all things by his Word?* And I am struck also that when he said this the angel did not say 'for with God no deed will be impossible', but 'no word'. Can he have said 'word' in order to let us understand that whereas men can easily say what they like, even when they are not able to put their words into effect, so just as easily and even incomparably more easily, can God do what men can only express in words? Let me clarify: if it was as easy for men to do, as to say, what they want, then it would also be true to say that with them no word is impossible. Now, since there is a saying, as true as it is well-known, that there is a great difference between saying and doing, at least for men, not for God, it follows that to God alone there is no word that is impossible, because doing and saying, saying and willing are all the same to him. For example: the prophets were able to foresee and foretell that a virgin and a barren woman would conceive and give birth. But they were never able to bring about this conception and this childbearing. But God, who gave them the power to foresee, could then easily prophesy by them whatever he wanted and can now, when he wants to, just as easily do what he promised. In God there is no difference between word and intention, for he is truth; nor is his act distinct from his word, for he is power; nor do means differ from deed, for he is wisdom. That was how it was that no word was impossible with God.

*Lk 1:37

*Wis 9:1

8. Virgin, you have heard what will happen, you have heard how it will happen. You have a double reason for astonishment and rejoicing. Rejoice, o Daughter of Sion, and be exceeding glad, Daughter of Jerusalem.* And since you have heard joyous and glad tidings, let us hear that joyous reply we long for, so that broken bones may rejoice.* You have heard what is to happen, I say, and you have believed. Believe also the way you have heard it is to happen. You have heard that you will conceive and bear a son;* you have heard that it will be by the Holy Spirit* and not by a man. The angel is waiting for your reply. It is time for him to return to the One who sent him.* We, too, are waiting for this merciful word, my lady, we who are miserably weighed down under a sentence of condemnation. The price of our salvation is being offered you. If you consent, we shall immediately be set free. We all have been made in the eternal Word of God, and look, we are dying.* In your brief reply we shall be restored and so brought back to life. Doleful Adam and his unhappy offspring, exiled from Paradise, implore you, kind Virgin, to give this answer; David asks it, Abraham asks it; all the other holy patriarchs, your very own fathers beg it of you, as do those now dwelling in the region of the shadow of death.* For it the whole world is waiting, bowed down at your feet. And rightly so, because on your answer depends the comfort of the afflicted, the redemption of captives, the deliverence of the damned; the salvation of all the sons of Adam, your whole race. Give your answer quickly, my Virgin. My lady, say this word which earth and hell and heaven itself are waiting for. The very King and Lord of all, he who has so desired your beauty,* is waiting anxiously for your answer and assent, by which he proposes to save the world.* Him whom you pleased by your silence, you will please now even more by your word. He calls out to you from heaven, 'O fair among women, let me hear your voice'.* If you let him hear your voice, then, he will let you see our salvation. Isn't this what you have been wanting, what you have been weeping for and

*Zech 9:9

*Ps 51:8

*Lk 1:31
*Lk 1:35

*Tob 12:20

*2 Cor 6:9

*Is 9:2

*Ps 45:11
*Jn 3:17

*Sg 1:7

sighing after, day and night, in your prayers? What
then? Are you the one who was promised, or must

*Mt 11:3

we look for another?* No, it is you and no one else.
You, I say, are the one we were promised, you are the
one we are expecting, you are the one we have longed
for, in whom your holy ancestor Jacob, as he was
approaching death, put all his hope of eternal life,

*Gen 49:18

saying, 'I shall wait for your salvation, Lord'.* You
are she in whom and by whom God our King himself
before all ages decided to work out our salvation in

*Ps 74:12

the midst of the earth.* Why hope from another for
what is now being offered to you? Why expect from
another woman what will soon be shown forth
through you, if you will only consent and say the
word? So, answer the angel quickly or rather, through
the angel, answer God. Only say the word and receive

*Jas 1:21

the Word: give yours and conceive God's.* Breathe
one fleeting word and embrace the everlasting Word.
Why do you delay? Why be afraid? Believe, give
praise and receive. Let humility take courage and
shyness confidence. This is not the moment for virginal simplicity to forget prudence. In this circum-
stance, alone, O prudent Virgin, do not fear
presumptuousness, for if your reserve pleased by its
silence, now much more must your goodness speak.
Blessed Virgin, open your heart to faith, your lips to
consent and your womb to your Creator. Behold, the

*Hag 2:8
*Rev 2:20

long-desired of all nations* is standing at the door and
knocking.* Oh, what if he should pass by because of
your delay and, sorrowing, you should again have to

*Sg 3:1-4

seek him whom your soul loves?* Get up, run, open!
Get up by faith, run by prayer, open by consent!

9. 'Behold,' she says, 'I am the handmaiden of the

*Lk 1:38

Lord; let it be to me according to your word'.*
Humility is always found in company with divine
grace, for 'God opposes the proud, but he gives grace

*Jas 4:6

to the humble'.* To prepare the throne of grace,
therefore, humility replied. 'Behold', she said, 'I am
the handmaiden of the Lord.' What is this humility
so sublime that it resists honor and refuses to vaunt
itself in glory? She is chosen to be the mother of

God, and she calls herself a handmaid. Surely this is a not insignificant sign of humility, when glory is proposed not to forget humility. It is no great thing to be humble when we are cast down, but honored humility is a great and rare virtue. If, miserable little man that I am, the Church should be deceived by my appearances and should honor me in any way, however slight (God allowing this for my sins and those of others), would I not immediately forget who I am and believe myself to be what men, who do not see my heart,* think I am? I believe public opinion, forget to look to my conscience and, not measuring honor by virtue, but rather virtue by honor, I think myself all the holier in that I occupy a higher post. You often see in the Church men who, having risen from low estate* to noble rank and from poverty to riches*, puff themselves up all of a sudden and, forgetting their original baseness, are ashamed of their own kith and kin because they are poor. And you see men greedy for money swoop to any church honors and soon come to flatter themselves they are holy because they have changed their robes if not their minds. They persuade themselves that they are worthy of the dignity they have attained through their ambition and—if I dare to say so—they owe more to their money than to their merits. I will say nothing of those who are blinded by ambition, and for whom honor is fodder for their pride.

*Jas 1:24

*1 Cor 1:26-28
*Ps 47:16

10. But here and there I see—and it gives me greater sorrow—people who, having scorned the pomp of this world, learn greater pride in the school of humility, and under the wings of their meek and humble Master* give themselves grander airs and become far more impatient in the cloister than they ever were in the world. And what is even worse, there are many in the house of God who cannot endure being slighted whereas, had they remained at home, they would have had to be slight. Many who would have merited no honors in the world, where they might aspire to them, now hanker to be honored here where honors are by one and all despised. I see still others—which ought to

*Mt 11:29

be the most painful sight—who having enlisted in
Christ's army involve themselves again in civilian
2 Tim 2:4   affairs and swamp themselves in greed for earthly
Sir 49:15   goods. They raise up great walls and let their morals
fall to pieces. Under pretext of the common good,
they barter their words to the rich and their cour-
tesies to ladies. They even, contrary to the edict of
their Emperor, covet their neighbor's goods and go
to court to reclaim their own, turning a deaf ear to
the Apostle who, by royal command, proclaims that
'to have lawsuits with one another is defeat. Why not
1 Cor 6:7   suffer wrong?' Is this the way they are crucified to
Gal 6:14   the world and the world to them, they who
formerly were scarcely known in their hamlet or
village and now run about the counties and frequent
the courts, on good terms with kings and hobnobbing
with princes? And what do I say about their habit,
which they choose more for its color than its comfort, cultivating elegant cut in vesture more than
virtue. I blush to say it, but fops with their dandy
ways are outdone when monks start buying clothes
for smartness. Heedless of any need, let alone
2 Tim 2:3   religious sentiment, these soldiers of Christ want
their habit to be an ornament rather than an
armament, and instead of preparing for battle and
Eph 2:2   the fight against the powers of the air as they
ought, with the insignia of poverty which would fill
their enemies with fear, they choose to sally out in
Mt 11:8   the soft raiment of peacetime and, defenseless, they
surrender without a scratch to the enemy. All these
evils only happen because, having renounced the
humility which made us leave the world, we chase
after the silly preoccupations of the world again, no
Pr 26:11   better than dogs who return to their vomit.

11. Whoever we are who are in such a state, let us
listen to the answer she gave, she who was chosen to
be the Mother of God, yet did not forget humility.
'Behold,' she said, 'I am the handmaid of the Lord;
Lk 1:38   let it be to me according to your word'. 'Let it be to
me' expresses desire, it does not signal doubt. Again,
the phrase 'let it be to me according to your word' is

to be understood more as the expression of a
yearner's affection than as a doubter's demand for
assurance. We may also, of course, take 'let it be' as a
prayer. No one prays for something unless he believes
in and hopes for it. God wills that we pray to him
even for those things which he has promised. It may
even be that he first promises many things which he
is disposed to give us so as to arouse our piety by his
promises and to urge us to procure by pious prayer
what he is ready freely to give us.* That is how the   *Mt 10:8*
gracious Lord,* who wills that all men should be   *2 Chron 30:9*
saved, wrests from us what we deserve and, while he
supplies us ahead of time with the very thing he is
going to grant, he acts freely lest he squander his gifts.
That is what the prudent Virgin understood when,
having already received the grace of a free promise,
she joined to it the merit of prayer saying, 'Let it be
to me according to your word'.* Let it be to me   *Lk 1:38*
concerning the Word according to your word. May
the Word who in the beginning was with God,*   *Jn 1:1*
become flesh of my flesh,* according to your word.   *Gen 2:23*
I beg that the Word be to me, not [a word] which
once pronounced fades away, but which conceived
remains, clothed with flesh* and not with air. Let it   *Job 10:11*
be to me, [a Word] not only audible to the ear, but
visible to the eyes, one which hands can touch* and   *Lk 24:39*
arms carry. And let it not be to me a written and
mute word, but one incarnate and living, that is to
say, not [a word] scratched by dumb signs on dead
skins, but one in human form truly graven, lively,
within my chaste womb, not by the tracings of a
dead pen, but by the workings of the Holy Spirit. Let
it be to me as it has never been to any person before
me and will be to no one after me.* For in many and   *Jn 1:15,27*
various ways God has spoken of old to our fathers by
the prophets,* and it is known that the word of the   *Heb 1:1*
Lord was put into the ear of some, into the mouth of
others and even into the hand of a few. But I ask that
it be to me in my womb according to your word. I
do not want it to be a word proclaimed to me in
discourse, symbolized in figures, or dreamed in the
imagination, but one silently inspired, personally

incarnate, corporally inviscerate. May the Word which
could not, and had no need to, be made in himself,
deign to be in me, deign to be to me according to
your word. Let it be for the whole world, but let it be
to me uniquely 'according to your word'.

I HAVE EXPLAINED the gospel reading as best I
can. I am aware that it will not please everyone, and
I know that I shall incur the censure of many who
are dissatisfied with it, and others will say I have
wasted time and been presumptuous in daring to try
my hand at explaining a passage which the Fathers
have already so fully explained. But as long as what
has been said since the Fathers is not contrary to the
Fathers, I see no reason why it should displease the
Fathers, or anyone else. If I have said what I have
learned from the Fathers, as long as the arrogance of
presumption does not stifle the fruit of devotion, I
will patiently listen to any talk of wasted effort.
Those who reproach me with having done something
otiose and unnecessary should realize, however, that
I did not so much intend to comment on the Gospel
as to seize from the Gospel an occasion for speaking
about something which it always gives me joy to
Job 10:14   speak about. If I have really sinned* by rousing my
own devotion rather than seeking the common good,
then the gracious Virgin can make excuses to her
merciful Son for my sin. Whatever its worth, I
dedicated this little work of mine most devotedly
to her.

ON THE PRAISES OF THE BLESSED MARY

EIGHT HOMILIES

BY

AMADEUS OF LAUSANNE

HOMILY I

EVERY HOLY and reasonable soul,* examining   *Cf. Rm 12:1
the secret mysteries of heaven and marking out
the rank of heavenly spirits, finds first after the
Redeemer the woman blessed among women, full of
grace,* the one who brought forth God yet did not   *Lk 1:28
lose the glory of her virginity. This blessed Virgin,
more brilliant than every light, more pleasing than
every sweetness, more eminent than every dominion,
lights up the whole world and renewing all things by
the pouring forth of her precious ointment* sur-   *Is 39:2,
passes the ranks of cherubim and seraphim both in   cf. Am 6:6
power and majesty. Therefore let the King, through
her glorious merits, admit us to his chamber* and   *Sg 1:3, 2:4
David's offspring, who shuts and no one opens,* will   *Rev 3:7 =
disclose to us his hidden secrets. He opens and no   Magnificat
one shuts. Let him reveal to us the joys of her who   antiphon for
bore him, the beauty of his chosen Mother.   20 December

    Moses and the prophets have borne witness to
her. Evangelists and doctors later took up the story
of her life, her habits and her grace, that the truth
might be consistently related and that what the first
had foretold should be the second might describe as
having been accomplished. Therefore, inspired by so
many illustrious persons, let us hasten towards that
odor of her perfumes and draw towards us the breath
of her graces. And while we are yet separated and
held back from the delight of beholding her, let us
rest among her flowers, on which in the Canticle she
bids us be supported, saying: 'Support me with
blossoms. Stay me with apples, for I am sick
with love.'*   *Sg 2:5

What are these flowers if not the divine mysteries in praise of her and the sacred mysteries once hidden from the world* which, now appearing in the flesh and manifested in the spirit,* have come forth from the sayings of the Fathers like buds from the trees. The Apostle explains these 'apples' by saying: 'The fruits of the spirit are love, joy, peace, patience, goodness, kindness, longsuffering, gentleness, faith, modesty, temperance, chastity.'*

She is supported with flowers when the oracles foretold are clear. She is stayed with apples when what was written comes to pass. 'Give her of the fruits of her hands and let her works praise her in the gates.'* But because the words treat of true flowers and the unfading fruit of justice, we must, aided by the gift of the Spirit, examine more closely those same flowers and fruits.

Let us notice therefore two golden baskets, as it were, filled with fruits and decked with flowers: the New Testament and the Old, standing on this side and on that, on the left hand and on the right of the Virgin. Of these the ancient one passes to the left and the new by grace shines on the right. For justly is the law of death on the left and the law of life on the right, for the former produces the sinner and the latter takes away sin. The Virgin of virgins herself is seen in springtime among the flowers and delighting in the sweetness of the fruits and, like the tree planted in the midst of paradise,* she raises her head to the height of heaven and, conceiving by the heavenly dew, brings forth the fruit of salvation, the fruit of glory, the fruit of life, and he who eats of it will live for ever.*

That what has been said may be clear, paradise is the garden to which the Church invites its beloved. 'Let my Beloved come into my garden and eat the fruit of her trees.'* She calls herself the garden of the beloved, she whom the Saviour's springs water,* the streams of his gifts inebriate, so that being wedded she rejoices in the love of the Spirit and, made fruitful by the drops of his dew,* she exults in the birth of many sons, as it were, in the profusion of

*Col 1:26
*1 Tim 3:16

*Gal 5:22-3

*Prov 31:31

*Gen 2:9, 3:3

*Gen 3:5,
 cf. Jn 6:59

*Sg 5:1
*Is 12:3

*Ps 65:10

her progeny. Here she calls the beloved to eat the
fruits of the trees, for she keeps for him fruits new
and old*, that is, the words of the two Testaments,   *Sg 7:13
or the perfect thoughts of her heart which serve for
her breasts, as one reads: 'Thy breasts shall be as the
grapes of the vine',* or surely all good spirits of   *Sg 7:8
angels and of men, some of whom persevere in newness of life, some grieve by reason of their age and of
their sin.

    By fruits new and old can also be meant the
Fathers new and old, among whom is nourished love
of the spouse until the day dawns and the shadows
fade.* Among these and in their midst rises the tree   *Sg 2:17
which we have called the tree of salvation, bearing the
food of life and the heavenly manna—manna pos-
sessing all delight and all sweetness,* and if the first   *Ws 16:20
Adam had touched it he would never have tasted
death. This bread the Son of Man in the Gospel
declares himself to be, saying: 'I am the living bread
who came down from heaven. If any man eats of this
bread, he will live for ever.'*   *Jn 6:51-2

    Let us therefore return to the baskets mentioned
before and let us consider the flowers on the left and
the fruits on the right. For what the Law promised in
the flowers, grace showed clearly in action, and there
is foretold what is to be. Here is praised virtue
brought to perfection. There is the sign, here the
actuality of the sign. Let us see the same baskets
representing the glory of Christ and the childbearing
of the Virgin. For this is the completion, this is the
end of the Testaments: to proclaim Christ, to show
forth Christ, to announce Christ, and the Virgin Mary.

    And that indeed is hidden under signs, now it is
cloaked in mysteries and metaphors, now celebrated
in festal rite, now disguised by sacrifices, now made
clear in prophecy or confirmed by the declaration of
the Gospel. And in this thicket of Lebanon*, on this   *1 Kg 10:17
thick shadowed mountain, there is revealed to us the
worthiness of the Spouse and the couch from which
he issues*, the Saviour of the world and the soil   *Ps 19:5
bringing forth the Saviour*, the star out of Jacob†,   *Is 45:8
the leader from Israel, the rod from the stem of   †Num 24:17

*Is 11:1
*Cf. Is 7:14

*Ps 47:5
Jesse, the flower from his root*. For in one place we read that Christ shall be born of a virgin,* will suffer in the flesh, will rise again in glory, will ascend in triumph,* will sit at the right hand of the Father and will bestow the gifts of the Spirit upon believers. In another place [we read] that he was born, suffered, rose, ascended and pours the gift of the Spirit upon his own.

Thus in the writings of truth it was announced of holy Mary that a virgin should conceive and a virgin should bring forth a son, his name Emmanuel,* His going forth should be from the beginning, from the days of eternity.* Him the virgin was worthy to conceive, she alone to bring forth, to suckle, amidst the prayers and ardent expectations of the Church as it prays and says: 'Who would give me you as my brother, sucking my mother's breasts, that I may find you without and kiss you and no one shall now despise me.'*

*Is 7:14

*Micah 5:2

*Sg 8:1

I shall find you, she says, without, in the light, you who are the Father's secret. I shall find you appearing in the flesh, who are hidden in invisible majesty. I shall find you, the bridegroom, coming forth from the marriage chamber,* who was conceived in the Virgin's womb by the Holy Spirit. And I shall kiss you in the flesh you have assumed, which is united to you. I shall kiss you, being joined to you in the partaking of your flesh and blood, so that no longer are we two but one flesh.* I shall kiss you, clinging to you in one Spirit, for he who clings to God is one spirit [with him].* And now no one will despise me. Not God the Father, seeing his own Son incarnate, not a holy angel adoring God made man, not a proud demon grieving that he has been defeated by Christ.

*Ps 19:5

*Gen 2:24,
  1 Cor 6:16

*1 Cor 6:17

For the rest, let us bring in some points from the Gospel. We read that the Virgin was saluted by the angel, espoused by God, that she conceived by the Holy Spirit,* brought forth true God and true man, who should save his people from their sins,* and of whose kingdom there should be no end.* He it is who was promised to Abraham, that in his seed all the nations should be blessed.* Of him the Apostle fitly

*Lk 1:26-38
*Mt 1:21
*Lk 1:33

*Gen 22:18

says: 'Behold how great is he'* who comes forth to save the nations. Truly great is he whom the Father sent into the world as his only begotten Son, whom the spiritual Virgin poured forth, whom a Virgin conceived and brought to birth, and after the birth remained a virgin.

Heb 7:4

He is announced by the archangel, conceived by the Holy Spirit, and is revealed by John while he was still enclosed within his mother's womb.* He is taken up by the aged Simeon with joy unspeakable and by him is foretold as the light of the nations and the glory of the people Israel.*

Lk 1:41

Lk 2:28-32

Do you therefore see how wisdom reaches boldly from end to end and disposes all things pleasantly?* From a child as yet unborn to a feeble old man it proclaims such consistent evidence and with such sweet harmony of truth plays upon the instruments. Hence it is said by the prophet: 'There is no one who can hide from its heat.'* He came forth from the Father, he returned to the Father. He went into hell, he returned to the throne of God. Who would be hidden from the heat of him whom an infant in the womb perceived, and by whom a chilled old man in the temple was set on fire? As if to signify that he willed to meet the Lord, the one rejoiced in what movement he could make. Taking into his arms Jesus whom he was awaiting with unspeakable longing, the other received divine love into the centre of his being, and not able to endure in his frail flesh the sweet warmth of the being who is above the heavens or in his frame the power of the firebearing word, he prayed for the dissolution of his body, that when his mortal habitation was destroyed he might enjoy more freely the sweetness he already tasted and might announce to those dwelling in the shadow of death* the birth of the Saviour whom he was proclaiming among those on earth.

Wis 8:1 = Magnificat antiphon for 17 December

Ps 19:6

Lk 1:79

But what are we doing or whither are we being carried? See, while we desire to extol her that was blessed among women,* we are praising the blessed fruit of her womb,* and while we seek to commend the beauty of the tree, we keep close to the

Lk 1:28
Cf. the 'Hail Mary'

surpassing beauty of the fruit. For every tree is known
by its fruit and is judged by its own yield.* As the
palm is assessed according to the sweetness of its
dates, the olive tree by the richness of the olives, the
wine by the juice of the grape, so the praise of the
Son enriches the Mother and the divine birth heaps
honor upon her that bore him.

It is pleasing, beloved, to repeat with another
meaning what has already been set forth and to con-
firm it by a fresh statement, so that blind unbelief
may be refused by the light, and faith in Christ reveal
itself clearly and without hindrance.

Let us therefore enter the Holy of Holies and gaze
upon the mercy seat, which has above it two cherubim
gazing upon it and overshadowing it as they face each
other with wings outstretched.* There among other
things shines the golden urn enclosing hidden manna.
There is Aaron's rod which budded.* Understand
that this is the mercy seat of which the Apostle says
that he is the propitiation for our sins.* The two
cherubim mean the two Testaments, for 'cherubim'
means the fulness of knowledge, and the fulness of
knowledge is in the Testaments. Rightly do the
cherubim cover the mercy seat which they gaze upon
as they face each other, for they conceal under figures
and riddles the Christ whom the Testaments agree in
proclaiming.

The golden urn is blessed Mary, golden by reason
of the excellence of her life, golden through her
integrity and purity, golden through the fulness of
grace. This urn held the hidden manna,* she who in
her sacred womb bore the bread of angels which
comes down from heaven* and gives life to the
world.

Further, the priestly rod signifies that same
glorious one who, descended from a priestly and
royal stock, gave birth to the King of saints, who is
a priest for ever after the order of Melchizedek.*
Truly is she called a rod for she is gracious and upright, sensitive and straight. Gracious through her
modesty and beauty, upright through her justice
and rectitude, sensitive through her capacity for

*Cf. Lk 7:20

*Cf. Ex 25:17-20

*Heb 9:4

*1 Jn 2:2

*Cf. Rev 2:17

*Cf. Jn 6:30,
Ps 78:24

*Ps 110:4, Heb
5:6,10 & 6:20

contemplation, straight through the merit of her life. She blossomed by the power of the Holy Spirit as Aaron's rod [blossomed] by miracle.* That rod put forth the fruit of the almond, she gave forth the finest almond, that has kernel and shell: kernel to restore, shell to protect. Kernel in his divinity, shell in his humanity.

*Num 17:8

Do you wish to know the kernel? Hear that 'in the beginning was the Word'.* Do you desire to know the shell? Hear: 'The Word was made flesh and dwelt among us.'* You see therefore that the kernel in the shell is the Incarnate Word. And since the shell has a rind, interpret the shell as the bitter woe of the flesh, the shell as the resurrection, the kernel as the divinity. By the rind Christ heals us, but the shell strengthens us [and] by the kernel ministers to us eternal life.

*Jn 1:1

*Jn 1:14

Let this kernel, this Word, again and again shed light upon us and bring us to his mother's chamber.* He who lives and reigns with God the Father in the Unity of the Holy Spirit, God through all ages. Amen.

*Cf. Sg 3:4

HOMILY II

SINCE WE HAVE, at the bidding of God, embarked upon the praises of the Blessed Virgin, it remains for us to complete her praise from the bottom of our heart and with dutiful voice. Let us gaze upon her glory and, entering the depth of so great a light, let us with swelling heart and unspeakable joy hasten through the vivid brightness of the paths, saying with Solomon, 'Her paths are lovely and all her ways are peaceful'.* What if, as the same prophet says, 'the path of the just, as a shining light, goes forth and grows into the perfect day'?* Who will be able to express the light and brightness of her paths? Yet we shall try to explain in part the progress and additions of her paths so that she may be perceived as glorious in her steps and be proclaimed in each of them.

*Prov 3:17

*Prov 4:18

For she possessed progress clearly marked and distinct growth, so that she advanced according to the fairest order of charity and,* going forward from virtue to virtue, she saw the God of gods in Sion,* being changed from glory to glory as by the Spirit of the Lord.*

*Sg 2:4
*Ps 84:7

*2 Cor 3:18

Firstly, therefore, she was deemed worthy to be adorned with the beauty of all the virtues. Secondly she was united to the Holy Spirit in a bond of wedlock. Thirdly, she was found the Mother of the Saviour. Fourthly, a sword pierced her soul and by the flesh taken of her flesh the ruin of the lost world is restored. Fifthly, she rejoices in her Son arising and ascending above the heaven of heavens to the right hand of the Father. Sixthly, she is caught up

69

from this world and as the Lord hastens to meet her
she is placed above the denizens of heaven. Seventh,
she will be completed when the fulness of the
Gentiles shall have entered and all Israel shall be

Rom 11:25-6 saved.* For beyond what it is right to be said or
believed, she rejoices in the general salvation of the
elect, knowing that it was for them that the Son of
God took flesh from her. Therefore she will then be
fulfilled, God providing a better thing, lest without

Heb 11:40 us she should not be made perfect.*

But now let us consider the names of those steps.
The first can be called justification or embellishment,
the second union or alliance, the third the Virgin
birth or new offspring, the fourth vigor of mind or
martyrdom, the fifth joy or wonder, the sixth
assumption or exaltation, the seventh fulness or perfection.

The aforesaid justification or embellishment proceeds from the fear of God. Union and alliance come
forth from an amazing piety. For the virgin birth and
the new offspring shed the light of knowledge upon
the universe. The work of fortitude was revealed in
the dying of Christ and his mother's watching it. But
when he arose the deep and unfathomable plan by
which he deceived the cunning foe and redeemed the
world poured forth into joy and wonder. Then when
the heavens are opened, invisible blessings are revealed, and something wonderous comes to pass, so
that, as God in man learned by experience the sufferings of man, so man taken up into God learns with
full understanding the glory of God. Finally wisdom
will bring fulfilment and perfection so that she will
appear perfect in the perfect and will exult in her
fulfilment.

Let us repeat what has been said and, lingering
again in those same steps, let us contemplate the
Lord, clinging to the ladder, and the angels ascending

Gen 28:12 and descending* towards the Virgin. For they marvel
at the pure maiden, the mother of the Lord, soon to
be the queen of heaven, and they break forth in
these words of wonder and praise: 'Who is she who

Sg 3:6 ascends in pure whiteness?'*

What is 'pure whiteness' if not adornment with white vesture? Adorned surely with the adornment of beauty and honor, of righteousness and holiness. The greatest of the prophets shone with the adornment of these garments when he said, 'I will rejoice greatly in the Lord and my soul will exult in my God, for he has clothed me with the garments of righteousness as a bridegroom adorned with a garland and as a bride with her jewels.'* Hence the psalmist says to God: 'Let your priests put on righteousness.'* But Isaiah exhorts Jerusalem to shake off the dust and be clothed with the garments of her glory.* And in reproach to the first angel it is said, 'You too have been a sign of the likeness in paradise of the delight of God. Every precious stone was your covering, sard, topaz, jasper, chrysolite, onyx, beryl, sapphire, carbuncle, and emerald.'* But we ought to know that these garments are white and fragrant, precious and diverse. White for innocence and purity and for the brightness of eternal light, fragrant for the perfume of esteem and good repute, precious because of their excellence and appropriateness, diverse because of their differing uses and varied shapes.

*Is 61:10
*Ps 132:9

*Is 52:2

*Ezk 28:12-13

Concerning the whiteness, it has already been said, 'Who is she who ascends in pure whiteness?'* And elsewhere we read, 'Who is she who goes forth as the rising dawn, beautiful as the moon, excellent as the sun?'* *As the dawn rising* from darkness to light, from error to faith, from the world to God, and in the faint gleam of her rising, tinged with the crimson of modesty, with the lovely pallor of humility. *Beautiful as the moon* because for ever remaining chaste, she is bathed in the brilliance of heavenly light and rejoices in its overshadowing. Everywhere brilliance, everywhere splendor, everywhere the whiteness of her garments is signified.

*Sg 3:6

*Sg 6:9

Of this whiteness other things might have been said, as that word of the Lord, who said concerning his own: 'They shall walk with me in white for they are worthy',* and 'He who has conquered shall be clothed in white garments'.* But we are hard pressed by our desire for brevity.

*Rev 3:4
*Rev 3:5

Now let us hear concerning the odor of the same garments the words of the bridegroom praising the bride in the marriage song: 'The odor of your garments is as the odor of incense.'* They say that by the odor of incense demons are put to flight, tears are evoked, God is appeased by intercessory tears. I would gladly have said that by the odor of Mary's virtues the angels of darkness are put to flight and are carried hither and thither by a kind of strong whirlwind, so that in them is fulfilled what was written, 'They became as the dust before the wind.'* That odor awakens those dead in their sins, strengthens feeble souls, urges on the good towards things better, and the better to things that are best. A good odor, which through the virgin called forth the king on his couch, so that coming to us he might receive what is ours, give us what is his, and establish, by unchanging law and unending peace, friendship with us. Thus therefore the fragrance of holy Mary's garments puts enemies to flight, attracts the good and placates God.

Concerning their richness and variety, in speaking to one lovely beyond the sons of men, the psalmist sings in praise of the bride saying, 'The queen stood at his right hand in vesture of God, clad in many hues,'* and a little afterwards he added, 'All the glory of the king's daughter is within, clothed with fringes of gold.'* Not only is she adorned with vesture of gold and golden fringes, but also with a covering which, as Solomon says, she made for herself.*

And she is covered with every precious stone.* For no gem, no precious stone, no rich pearl is lacking from her covering, until no longer can it be called [just] rich, but justly rich beyond all richness. For just as one richness, spreading in a moment or rather every moment of a moment and part of a moment produces many riches, so many converge into one so that they become one by sharing in one. And this richness is charity, the bridal robe, the robe without spot or wrinkle,* the robe that cannot be torn, without seam, woven in one piece.* From this, through this and in this* are all things dear, whatever things are good. And they are all one in unity, the

*Sg 4:11

*Ps 35:5

*Ps 45:9

*Ps 45:14

*Prov 31:22
*Ezk 28:13

*Eph 5:27
*Jn 19:23
*Rm 11:36

same in identity, simple in simplicity. In the whole
they hold the whole and in the whole they rejoice
far removed from any lessening or increase, from any
diversity or multiplicity.

We have spoken about the richness of the ornaments. Let us now discuss their variety, some examples of which we set forth above. Of this there are
two kinds, one of color, the other of use.

This variety which exists in color is divided into
white and black, red and green. These are said to be
the primary colors and these in particular adorn the
aforesaid garment. It is green as the olive or laurel
and as the rainbow showing green in the clouds. It is
green in the faith and hope of the eternal, in obedience to the commandments, in the contemplation of
eternal greenness and the greenness of eternity. It is
red like a fiery globe, as a king's purple,* as a   *Sg 7:5
twice-dyed scarlet* cloth betokening the love of   *Ex 25:4
God and of one's neighbor. Its black is like horn and
like buds of palm trees, or else surely like painted
ivory and like a still heaven at midnight. That color is
set as the foundation and it underlies the other colors
so that it signifies to us that the virtue of humility
should be laid down as a foundation. If we seek for
whiteness, it shines by means of perpetual virginity
and perfect purity. Also by the charm of its beauty
it turns back the mighty rhinoceros and attracts the
God of majesty. Many other things of spiritual meaning can be found by the spiritual on the subject of the
variety and meaning of the colors.

But variety which suitably serves for use shines
forth also in many ways. For some ornaments cover
and adorn the lofty head and neck of the blessed one,
some her hair and ears, some her breast and arms,
some her hands and fingers. Some of them clothe
her whole body, some encircle her thighs, some
protect her feet.

Her head signifies her mind. For just as the head
controls the body's members, so the mind rules and
controls the feelings of the soul. In the neck, which
towers over the other members and supplies to the
limbs vital power, is expressed her loftiness, by which,

presiding over the members of the Church, she unites the head to its body, for she unites Christ with the Church and the life which in the first place she received she pours forth on her other members. For it was fitting that just as death entered the world through a woman, so through a woman did life enter.* And as in Eve all died, so in Mary all rose again.* She—Eve—sinfully credulous of the serpent's words mixed the poisonous draught of death. She—Mary—bruising the serpent's head,* served to all the antitoxin of life, so she slew death and restored life.

*Cf. Rom 5:12
*1 Cor 15:22

*Gen 3:15

The hairs of her head are the thoughts of her heart, her ears the inner hearing. In her breast lies hid her secret and her thought stirs. Hence this custom has grown up that the guilty beat their breasts and, as it were, in striking accuse their own unrighteousness. By the breast therefore the secrets of that glorious breast are signified, by the arms the virtues of her works, by the hands the works themselves, by the fingers divers kinds of works. Her body is the undivided unity of her works, her thighs her desires, her feet her affections by which, entering upon the paths of justice, she has left behind clear footprints for those coming after.

Her feet are shod in the skins of dead beasts because they are protected by the examples of the Fathers who have gone before. The thighs are girt with the girdle of righteousness and with the belt of praise.* The body is clothed with that garment of which the Apostle says, 'As many of you as have been baptized in Christ have put on Christ.'* And he exhorts us to put on the new man who has been created after God in righteousness and the holiness of truth.*

*Is 11:5

*Gal 3:24

*Eph 4:24

Observe, man, and be amazed at a renewal so great, when Jeremiah says, 'The Lord will create a new thing upon the earth, a woman alone shall enclose a man.'* The same woman who enclosed has been enclosed. Enclosing the flesh, she has been enclosed by the Spirit. Enclosing the new man, she has been enclosed by the new man. Enclosing as generating, enclosed as regenerated. Generating in the

*Jer 31:22, cf.
Bernard, Miss
2,8

shape of humanity, regenerated in the shape of renewal.

Let us pass on to the rest. Rings adorn her fingers because each one of her works shines forth in faith and love. Now a ring betokens faith and pure love. Her hands are beautifully shaped, golden, filled with hyacinths.* Beautiful because of the perfection of her work, golden because of the brightness of her wisdom, filled with hyacinths because of her pure and fervent intention. For the hyacinth, blue and red, reveals her shining and fervent work. *Sg 5:14

Her arms are stamped with that seal of which the bridegroom says in the Canticle, 'Set me as a seal upon thy arm.'* Surely the fiery law covers the right hand and her left shines bright with the purple of the Lord's passion. From her ears hang the earrings of obedience, the fillet of discipline binds her hair, chains of purest and clearest thought adorn her breast, a golden necklace is at her throat. With this those in second place in kingdoms are wont to be crowned and this is the second crown. For the first gleams on the awesome head of the ruler of the whole world. The second has fallen to the lot of his mother. For she reigns uniquely in the kingdom of God and Christ.* Then under her and after her are the highest saints. *Sg 8:6

*Eph 5:5

Her head is covered with the glory of her virginity and is veiled in the scarlet of charity. The blessing of the Lord is upon it and it is filled with the blessings of all nations.* It is crowned also with the crowns of all peoples and goes forth to the rejoicing of all. See in the beauty of her diadem the assembly of saints exulting in her quivering and reflecting light. See in the carved stones, the shining jewels, the glittering stars, the prophets awaiting her, the martyrs triumphant, confessors and virgins rejoicing. That crown is red with roses, white with lilies, pale with violets, green with laurels, heavy with palms, rich in oil, filled with every fruit, packed with every sweetness. *Gen 27:29

Let it suffice that we have said these things, beloved, concerning the justification or adornment of the Virgin. It remains that by her holy leading we should be prepared to treat of deeper matters and more secret mysteries leading us to the vision of God.

HOMILY III

LORD, we have heard your works and we have been astounded.* We have pondered your marvels and we have fainted.* As your Word descended, our heart has been melted* and all our innermost being, trembling, has been laid bare to him. For while silence held all things and night in her journey reached her mid-course, your Almighty Word came from its royal abode.* You poured out, o Father, the tenderness of your love upon us* and you could no longer contain the multitude of your mercies.* You shed light in the darkness, dew upon the dryness and in the bitter frost you kindled a raging fire.

*Hab 3:2

*Cf. Ps 119:18
*Cf. Jos 7:5

*Wis 18:14-15
*Lk 1:78
*Ps 51:1

Your Son appeared to us as an abundance of food when grievous famine threatened, as a spring of living water to a life in distress and fainting from thirst in the heat. Or surely just as there is wont to appear a strong helper and deliverer for men beseiged,* who are about to rush out into battle with death before their eyes, with the enemy's threatening sword and his armed right hand thirsting for blood, so He appeared for us and became our salvation.*

*Cf. Ps 70:5, 71:7

*Is 12:2

Yet it is an excellent and salutary thing to recount again the beginning of our salvation and to treat of his incarnation, to recall whence he came, in what sort he descended, where and how he was conceived. We put last the manner of his conception so that following our plan through we may discuss more fully that ineffable union by which the womb of Blessed Mary bore fruit of the Holy Spirit. For though it be ineffable, yet much joy, a wondrous astonishing sweetness, can be richly drawn from it.

For there is the sum total of our faith, there the
honor of our existence, the root of our life, the light
of knowledge, the unbreakable bond of love and the
door open to the eternal.

Now let blessed David present himself to us and
tell us whence He came. His going forth was from the
Ps 19:6   highest heaven. What does 'from highest heaven'
mean? From God, who is the supreme being, the
highest good, the utmost blessedness.

He is the supreme being who is neither limited by
place nor subject to change nor enclosed within
time. But he limits all things by the immensity of his
majesty, moves all things mutable by his own immu-
tability, encloses all times within the infinity of his
eternity.

The supreme good is the same being, a being not
derived from another, a good not from another good;
not only because of the aforesaid immensity, immu-
tability and eternity, but also because of the eternal
bounty of the creation which it brought forth in
time. And because of the infinite wisdom by which
before anything was, it disposed all things in eternity.
And because of the love ineffable by which his work
was embraced before it was brought forth in creation.

Again, supreme blessedness consists in supreme
good and by the reception of itself produces the
truly blessed. For by participation in this blessedness eternal life is gained, perfect wisdom is granted,
the fulness of love is possessed, so that there is complete freedom from care in eternity of life, full enjoy-
ment in the light of wisdom, complete sanctity in the
sweetness of love. These things we have said concerning supreme being, supreme good and supreme
blessedness, that the height of heaven from which
Christ came may shine upon us.

But because this highest heaven is the Father, the
highest heaven the Word and the highest heaven the
Holy Spirit, Christ came from the Father, he came
also in a way from the Word, he came from the Holy
Spirit. But in what way did he come from the Father,
he who never left the Father? How from the Word, he
who never ceased to be the Word? How from the

Holy Spirit when the Holy Spirit* proceeds from the   *reading* spiritus
Father and himself. This is a difficult question and   *for* spiritu
demands deep thought.

And what shall be our path to these holy mysteries of God? In what order shall we complete the
journey we have begun? Look, a thick mist and a
luminous cloud impedes our ways. That water which
holy Ezekiel saw issuing from the temple, covering
not only his heels and knees but loins and neck, is
poured over us to prevent our crossing.* Yet he in   *Ez 47:1
in whom we hope is present; in him we have from our
youth up been taught to trust, that he would flood
our souls and raise us above ourselves, setting our
feet like harts' feet,* to bring us beyond our own   *Hab 3:19,
heights, establishing for us a watch tower on the   Ps 18:33
mount with Moses and Elijah* so that we may be able   *Mt 17:3
to behold with unveiled face that which we seek.*   *2 Cor 3:18
There shall be shown that it is good to be there;
there we shall be more fully instructed concerning
the vision of God.*   *Mt 17:4
But if we are willing to approach the darkness in
which he himself is, having entered into the midst of
the cloud,* stirred by the glory of such majesty,   *Ex 24:18
dismayed also by the immensity of that infinity, we
shall not stand fast, we shall be as nothing. For God
dwells in light inaccessible;* his fire devours the flesh   *1 Tim 6:16
like stubble;* his face no man can see and live.†   *Is 5:24
The angels cannot fathom his depth; no power comes   †Ex 33:20
near to him except that which was united to the Word
in the unity of Person. Therefore let us give glory to
God and, falling on our faces, let us adore from afar
the traces of the Trinity, believing in our hearts and
confessing with our lips,* for whatever we have   *Rom 10:10
thought or said concerning him is less than he is.

Protected by this faith, let us turn back to solve
the question before us. Christ has come from the
Word, he has come from the Holy Spirit, since the
whole Trinity accomplished his conception and his
incarnation. For to come from the highest Trinity
was no other than to be conceived and to become a
human being by the same Trinity. Therefore it was
said, 'His going forth is from the highest heaven.'*   *Ps 19:6

The Only-begotten came from the Father and from himself according to another kind of reasoning as well. He came from the Holy Spirit—in one way, however, from the Father and himself, in another way from the Holy Spirit.

Begotten of the Father eternally, begotten in time he came forth from his mother, remaining invisibly with the Father and dwelling visibly with men. For to go forth from the Father was this: to enter upon our world, to be seen openly, and to become what, from the nature of the Father, he was not. This indeed is wonderful, he came from him from whom he did not depart, going forth from him with whom he stayed, so that without intermission he was wholly in eternity, wholly in time; wholly was he found in the Father when wholly in the virgin, wholly in his own majesty and in his Father's at the time when he was wholly in our humanity.

If you ask how, gather the truth by means of an illustration. A word conceived in the heart goes forth complete in the voice, so that it comes perfectly to others, yet remains wholly in the heart. So the good Word spoken forth from the heart of the Father went forth into the broad plain, yet did not leave the Father.

*Jn 1:14
*Ph 2:7

The Word also came from himself and came down beneath himself and dwelt among us,* when he emptied himself, taking the form of a servant.* That emptying was a descent. Yet he descended in such a way that he did not lose himself. He was made flesh in such a way that he did not cease to be the Word, nor did the taking of* humanity lessen the glory of his majesty.

*assumptio

We must also know in what way he came from the Holy Spirit, since the Holy Spirit proceeds from him. The Holy Spirit indeed proceeds from him by an eternal procession, but he, born of the Virgin Mary, came from the Holy Spirit by a temporal conception. Concerning the eternal procession the psalmist says, 'By the word of the Lord were the heavens established and all the power of them by the breath of his mouth'.* The Word of the

*Ps 33:6

Father he calls the mouth of the Lord, by which once God spoke to us.* He called the breath of his mouth Holy Spirit in that it comes forth from his mouth.

That the Word came forth from the Holy Spirit, you have it thus in Habakkuk: 'God will come from the south wind and the holy one from Mount Paran.'* By 'south wind', in which is life-giving warmth and generative power, is meant the spirit which brings newness of life, making the seeds of virtue come forth. And though blessed Jerome, whom we desire to follow, calls Mount Paran the Father,* yet by Mount Paran the same Lord [the Holy Spirit] is meant. He is called mountain because of his preeminent charity, Paran because of the distribution of his graces. For 'Paran' is by interpretation 'division'. And the spirit of the Lord divides his gifts to each one as he wills.* Therefore, God came from the south wind, because he was conceived from a life-giving and regenerating warmth. He came from Mount Paran because he poured forth from an ineffable loftiness the divisions of charisms.

Tell us, holy Daniel, how he came down from this mountain. 'A stone,' he says, 'was cut without hands from the mountain.'* What stone? 'The stone which the builders rejected.'* A cornerstone, the stone which Jacob anointed, a stone in which there are seven eyes.* This was hewn without hands from the mountain, because the holy virgin conceived him not from a man nor by means of man, but by the Holy Spirit.

Tell us also, blessed David, how he descended. 'He shall come down as rain upon the fleece, and as drops that water the earth.'* First one must say what this fleece is, what the earth [is], then how the rain descended on the fleece and how the drops watered the earth.

A fleece, although it comes from the flesh, grows outside the flesh and knows not the sufferings of the flesh. By its softness, its homely color, it proclaims its gentleness and humility. Also, by being easy to handle it bears the mark of simplicity and innocence

*Heb 1:2
*spirit = breath

*Hab 3:3

*In Abac. 2; PL 25:1374B

*1 Cor 12:11

*Dan 2:34
*Ps 118:22

*Eph 2:20, Gen 28:18, Zach 3:9

*Ps 72:6

and with its natural covering it keeps warm the delicate limbs. It betokens the glorious Virgin, who dwelling in flesh, raised herself beyond the flesh and slew the passions of the flesh by the power of the Spirit. For she is known to have lived like no other in gentleness and humility. No one will be able adequately to describe her simplicity and innocence. The understanding does not grasp the charity by which she protects and unceasingly cherishes the human race.

Further, the aforesaid 'earth' points to the same Virgin, called 'earth' because of a certain likeness. For just as the old Adam was formed from an earth *Gen 2:7* uncorrupt,* that had suffered no contagion, so the virgin soil brought forth from the earth a new Adam.

If you do not believe me when I proclaim the rising of the new man from the earth, believe the psalmist when he says 'truth has sprung from the *Ps 85:11* earth'.* What greater newness [can there be] than the arising from the earth of the one who is the Truth? Believe also the trumpet of Isaiah as it produces a sweet and tuneful sound, saying 'drop down, O heavens, from above and let clouds rain upon the the just. Let the earth open and bring forth a *Is 45:8* Saviour.'* Again, he says, 'There will be a seed of the Lord in magnificence and glory and a lofty fruit of *Is 4:2* the earth.'* The seed of the Lord stood forth in magnificence and glory when, conceived by the Holy Spirit, sprung from the root of Jesse, it *Cf. Ezk 7:10* blossomed in full on the very top of the rod,* or rather it was the blossom. 'And the spirit of the Lord rested upon him, the spirit of wisdom and understanding, the spirit of counsel and strength, the spirit of knowledge and godliness, and the spirit *Is 11:2-3* of the fear of the Lord filled him.'* The fruit of the earth was raised on high because the blessed fruit of Mary was worthy to be lifted to the very heights of the godhead. We have said these things that we may show that the word 'earth' may be understood as Mary.

It remains to discuss how the rain descends upon the fleece and how the drops flow out over the earth.

The rain descends upon the fleece without sound, without movement, without any cleavage or division. It is gently poured out, peacefully received, sweetly drunk. Thus the drops gradually, little by little spread over the earth falling down so wonderfully and so gently that their coming is scarcely perceived and as they depart they bring forth the shoots. In the same way the rain coming from beyond, above the heavenly waters, came down into the Virgin's womb without human act, with no movement of concupiscence, her integrity unimpaired, her virgin's doors still locked. Gently was it poured, calmly received, ineffably made flesh. It came drop by drop upon her soil, unseen as it entered, and as it departed plainly going forth.

There are still other pictures of so great an event. For just as the sun's brightness penetrates glass without breaking it, and as a glance of the eyes plunges into calm clear water without parting or dividing it, while it opens up all things to their very depth, so the Word of God drew near the Virgin's dwelling and went forth from it, her virgin womb still closed. For he who might easily have created from nothing a body apart from the Virgin could easily draw without lesion of the flesh a body taken from the Virgin. For he did not submit to the law of nature but subjected the law of nature to himself.

We have told how the Word of God came down. Where he came down is made clear in like manner, for he came down into the Virgin's womb, a womb unstained, unspotted, hallowed by the touch of divine unction. There, united to our flesh, made akin to our nature, he wrought a most holy and secret mystery, that the two might be in the one flesh and enjoy the one dwelling.*

*Cf. Gen 2:24

Therefore the invisible God was made visible man, the impassible and immortal showed himself passible and mortal. He who was not confined within the garments of our substance willed to be so confined. There is enclosed within the womb of a mother one whose immensity encloses the whole range of heaven and earth. And Mary's body enfolds him whom the heaven of heavens does not contain.

If you ask how it was done, hear the archangel setting forth the plan to Mary, and saying to her, 'The Holy Spirit shall come upon you and the power of the Most High shall overshadow you.'* Rejoice therefore and be glad, Mary, for you will conceive by a breath. Rejoice, for you will be found pregnant by the Holy Spirit.* You had indeed been betrothed to Joseph, but you were forestalled by the Holy Spirit. He who created you marked you and claimed you for himself. He who fashioned you himself became your spouse; he became the lover of your beauty, he who fashioned it. He himself calls you, saying 'Come, my friend, my fair one, my dove. For now the winter is past and departed. Come.'* He desired your beauty† and longed to join you to himself. Impatient of delay, he hastens to come to you.

Rise, therefore, put on your garments of glory.* Adorn yourself with your precious jewels, for the Lord has pleasure in you.* Rise to meet your bridegroom and your God and say to him, 'Behold, the handmaid of the Lord'.* Hasten, delay not, for he will not tarry* but will rejoice as a giant to run his course.* Do you hasten too, forget your own people and your father's house,* run to meet him that you may be kissed with the kiss of God* and be caught up in his blessed embrace.

Go forth, for already the bridal couch has been placed and the bridegroom comes to you, the Holy Spirit comes. He will come upon you and the power of the Most High will overshadow you.* Suddenly, while you do not hope for it, while you grieve for the ills of delay and are distressed by the absence of the beloved, swiftly and suddenly he will come upon you that you may enjoy unexpected bliss and be overwhelmed with a new gladness.

He will come not only upon you but into you, that he may see you more closely and breathe into you a grateful love, bringing into you with an intimate bedewing the good word, the word full of happiness and wonder, full of counsel, full of joy, full of salvation. 'The Holy Spirit will come upon

Lk 1:35

Mt 1:18

*Sg 2:10-11
†Cf. Ps 45:11*

Cf. Is 52:1

Is 62:4

Lk 1:38
Hab 2:3
Ps 19:5
Ps 45:10
Sg 1:1

Lk 1:35

you,' that at his touch your womb may tremble, your belly swell, your spirit rejoice, your stomach expand. 'Be blest', that is, increase the more,* you who enjoy such sweetness, you are worthy of such a heavenly kiss, you are united to such a spouse, you are made fruitful by such a bridegroom.

*macta *i.e.* magis aucta

'The Holy Spirit shall come upon you.' He has come to others of the saints, he will come to others, but he comes more to you, for he chose you before and above all others, that you may surpass all those who have been before or after you or shall be in the fulness of grace.

He filled Abel with such innocence that, pure in deed and gentle at heart,* he suffered death at his brother's hand.* But your innocence has restored thousands of guilty ones to innocence and salvation. He translated Enoch,* but the flesh which you will bear, when it has been taken up from the earth, will draw all things to itself.* He filled Abraham with faith and an obedience that should profit his descendants,* but, saved by your faith and obedience, the whole world gives thanks. He filled Moses and he appointed him to be the one to bring the Law,* not grace, but you are the one bringing not only the Giver of the Law but the Bestower of grace and glory.* He appointed David prophet and king,* but David writes for you and calls your Son his Lord.* Why should I say more? You surpass all, you rank not only before all humanity but even before heaven's highest powers.

*Ps 24:4

*Gen 4:8

*Gen 5:24

*Jn 12:32

*Gen 22

*Ex 19

*Jn 1:17
*1 Sam 16
*Ps 110:1

Hence you will inherit a name more glorious than theirs. For while one is called 'angel of God', another 'prophet', another 'herald' and each is valued according to his name, in proportion to his rank and dignity, you will be called by the unique and special name 'Mother of God', and therefore mother of salvation, mother of grace, mother of mercy.

'The Holy Spirit will come upon you.' He will come in fertility, in abundance, in fulness, in the outpouring of flesh and spirit. And when he has filled you, he will still be over you and will be borne upon your waters to create in you a better and a

greater wonder than when in the beginning he was
borne upon the waters to bring creation to beauty

*Gen 1:2

and shape.*

'And the power of the Most High shall overshadow

*1 Cor 1:24

you.' Christ, the power and the wisdom of God* shall
overshadow you. He will take from you his humanity
and in the taking of the flesh he will keep the fulness

*Col 1:19

of the divinity* which you could not carry. He will
overshadow you because the humanity taken by the
Word will expose itself to the light inaccessible and
that light, controlled by the exposure, will flood your
chaste body.

Pleasant is it, beloved, to linger awhile amidst such
solemnity of joy and to inquire a bit about the aforesaid conception. Pleasant it is, addressing her, to
question the divine enclosure, the most precious and
holy vessel in which the Word of God was conceived.

We pray you therefore, Lady, most worthy Mother
of God, not to scorn those who seek in fearfulness,

*Cf. Mt 7:7-8

ask in piety, knock in love.* We ask, by what feeling
you were moved, by what affection held, by what
incitement stirred when these things took place in
you and you conceived the Word made flesh. Where
was your soul, your heart, your mind, your feeling,
your reason? You were on fire like the bush which
once was shown to Moses and you were not burnt

*Ex 3:2

up.* Being melted, you burned with supernal fires.
Melted in the fire, you took strength from the fire
so that you even burned and again you melted.

The fire revealed a shining dew, the shining dew
produced an anointing, the anointing furnished the
holy seed by which Abraham was promised that in it

*Gen 22:17-18

all nations should be blessed.* You have clung,
beauteous virgin, in close embrace to the author of
beauty and were made more a virgin, indeed more
than a virgin, because mother and virgin, you received
by the inpouring of God this holy seed. Therefore

*Lk 1:28

hail, full of grace, the Lord is with you.* Blessed are
you among women and blessed the fruit of

*Lk 1:42

your womb.*

HOMILY IV

YESTERDAY, beloved, our discourse—concerned with spiritual union and the virgin conception—is hastening towards the birth, so that we declare that she whom we know to have conceived by the Holy Spirit brought forth true God and man. For in labor she brought forth the Son of God, so that God came down into her body wondrously deeming her worthy, wondrously and incredibly loving her, and in the flesh that he took he visited the orphaned sons of Adam.

Therefore the Son of God was made the son of man. In unity of the person he was God and man: God of the substance of the Father, begotten before the world; man of the substance of his mother, born in the world. So, a giant of twin substance, he rejoiced to sing with tuneful voice and sweet airs to the lyre of our body and on the organ made of our flesh to send forth dulcet sounds to re-echo as it were with ineffable harmony, so that he raised up stones, moved trees, drew wild beasts, led forth on high men delivered from their flesh.

For by the sweetness of his wonderful song he raised up from stones sons of Abraham and the trees of the wood, that is the hearts of the Gentiles, he moved to faith.* Wild beasts also, that is fierce passions and savage barbarism, he tamed to good ways and he set among the gods men drawn from among men. Well did David, whose songs echo to the ends of the earth, fulfil the role of singer, for from his stock was that greater precentor to be born.

But now let us see how the blessed virgin gave him

*Mt 3:9

birth. She bore him with her virginity untouched,
because she conceived him with her modesty preserved. She was inviolate when she brought him
forth, untouched as she conceived him. And him
whom she conceived without sin she gave birth to
without pain. Having no contact in her conception,
she suffered no tearing at his birth. For if (what is
wrong to imagine) she had conceived him in the lust
of the flesh, doubtless she would suffer pain at his
=RB 7:33   birth, as Scripture says, 'lust involves pain'.*

Our first parent [Eve], disregarding the true and
eternal joy which she could have enjoyed by the love
and contemplation of God, fell, weakened by the
dissolute lust of the flesh and through shameful
intemperance she endured the ills of suffering and
the stings of cruel death. Hence comes it that to this
day the daughters of Eve bring forth in pain and
what they conceived in delight they put forth with
great bitterness of the flesh.

But not only they, but all the sons of Adam who
delight in the flesh, are tormented in the flesh, so
that the source of their torment is their delight. And
they experience in pain what they had previously
taken with delight and they learn not to love the
flesh nor to fulfil its desires. 'For he who has sown
in the flesh,' says the Apostle, 'shall from the flesh
Gal 6:8   reap corruption.'* Further, the Mother of God, not
delighted by the flesh nor tormented in the flesh, was
the more virgin by her conception and was the
stronger by giving birth at the hand of that midwife
concerning which the psalmist said to God, 'Let it be
Ps 119:73   Your hand that saves me'.*

The only-begotten of the Father is called the
Heb 1:2   hand of God, through whom he made the world.*
This hand, having been made, when it became incarnate not only inflicted no wound upon the mother
but, as the prophet bears witness, itself bore our
Is 53:4   griefs and carried our sorrows.* Clearly that hand
was full of remedies, full of medicines; it healed every
ill, drove away deaths and awakened those that were
dead, broke up the gates of hell, bound the strong
one and stripped him of his armor, opened the

heavens and poured out the spirit of charity upon the
hearts of his own.* That hand looses those that are
bound, enlightens the blind, raises those struck down,
loves the righteous, protects strangers, supports the
orphan and the widow.* It snatches the tempted from
temptation, restores with consolation those who
sorrow, brings back joy to the sad, protects under its
shadow those who toil, writes for those who reflect
upon the laws, touches and blesses the hearts of those
who pray, that by its touch they may be
strengthened in love, by its blessing they may make
progress and persevere in their work. And thereafter
he brings them back to their fatherland and leads
them to the Father.

For this cause was the Word made flesh, that by
the flesh it might draw the flesh and that joining
flesh to flesh by the bond of charity it might bring
back the wandering sheep to the invisible things of
God and to the invisible omnipotent Father.* Because
deserting God, that sheep fell in the flesh it needed by
the mystery of this incarnate hand to be lifted up and
returned to the Father as in a sort of carriage.

Therefore with this midwife hand, Mary not only
felt no pain but remained virgin even in giving birth.
She is the door concerning which we read in the book
of Ezekiel: that door will remain closed for the
prince and through it the prince will go forth.*
Through this door Christ, prince of the kings of the
earth,*indeed has issued and just as in entering he did
not open it, so in leaving he did not unclose it. He
passed through in peace, and his path was not seen.

But if you marvel that God was born while Mary's
womb remained closed and sealed with her virgin
purity, marvel also that though the door of the
sepulchre was closed and sealed, he returned to the
upper world, and when the doors were locked came in
to his disciples.* For we are not removing your
wonder, but keeping at bay your unbelief.

Whatsoever he willed, the Lord did,* and all his
works may be wondered at but not examined. 'All
things are difficult,' said Solomon, 'and man cannot
explain them in words.'* For, not to mention how

*Mt 4:23-4 &
  12:29

*Ps 146:8

*Cf. Lk 15:5-6

*Ezk 44:2-3

*Rev 1:5

*Jn 20:19

*Ps 135:6

*Qo 1:8

from one small grain a mighty forest of trees arises
and how from the seed of Adam and Eve was
produced the mass of humanity, who would explain
the springing of insects from the earth? Whence came
the spreading of their wings, the march of their
feet? Whence the eyes and shape of the head?
Whence the shape of the body? Whence the sting so
fine that sometimes it disappears from the sight? It is
so hollow and pierced that when the blood has been
taken in the tiny body of a creature so short-lived
is filled.

But if your reason collapses at the examination of
an insect, o man, be ashamed to search into matters
higher than yourself and to track down matters
stronger than you. If you do not reflect on yourself
and the depth of your soul, how do you rise to the
infinite majesty? How will the man who does not
know how to count to the first number be able to
judge of arithmetic? Will the man who does not
know what a point is or a line be proficient in
geometry? Will the one who does not know how to
utter a sound be able to teach music? Will the man be
a skilled astronomer who does not know what movement is? So he who does not know himself does not
penetrate the deep things of God.

Yet what is human wisdom compared with the
wisdom of God? It holds in its presence neither the
place of a point nor the point of a point. If I may
put forward a surprising idea, the insect's eye can be
compared somewhat proportionally with the immensity of heaven, but the measure of man is out of all
proportion to the divine immensity. What part in
infinity has the finite, the measurable in the im-
measurable, that which lasts but a moment with the
eternal? Or by what multiplication or number will the
creature be compared with the Creator? If you
stretch a thousand thousand into infinity, you will
exhaust yourself in fruitless toil, and not even
in the very smallest proportion will you be able to
compare human knowledge with divine wisdom.

If therefore the being of God is reflected upon,
there will not be found the substance of man.

Witness the prophet, who says, 'All the peoples are in your presence as though they are not and are counted as a moment and mere emptiness.'* And the Lord said to Moses, 'This will you say to the sons of Israel: "He who is has sent me to you." '* When he said that he is, he took away being from others.

*Is 40:17

*Ex 3:14

Therefore believe God, human insignificance—or rather the nothingness of humans—and let the firm foundation of your reasoning be upon All powerful wisdom. Set that forth, take up that and from that draw your conclusion.

Believe that all those who attach themselves perfectly to their Creator will not be thwarted by the law of nature but will be established above nature by nature's Creator. Nature did not impose its law upon its Creator but the Creator gave to nature the laws he willed. And when he wills, he changes the laws themselves, as when he made wine from water and fashioned eyes from clay.* When too, holding his very self in his hands he shared it with his disciples to be eaten and drunk,* remaining wholly outside them and feeding inwardly those who ate it. So, as to the argument, he went forth from the closed womb of the Virgin. These things have been said against the unbelievers and for the benefit of unbelievers.

*Jn 2:11, 9:6

*Cf. Mt 26:26

I will not leave untouched you, the Jews, who killed the prophets sent to you and slaughtered the Son of God who had come for your salvation,* mixing the same cup for the Lord of the prophets as you had mixed before for the prophets. For you said, 'This is the heir. Let us kill him and the inheritance will be ours.'* But because you killed the heir, you lost the inheritance. No longer should it be called your inheritance. You lost it after the space of a thousand years.

*Cf. Mt 23:37

*Mt 21:38

Why then do you say that the Messiah has not yet come, that the Christ has not yet been born? Either you yourselves are lying or you make a liar of the Truth which speaks in the psalm concerning David, saying, 'I will establish his seed for ever and his

*Ps 89:29
*Ps 89:35-7
*Gen 44:10
*Si 39:14
*Ps 110:1
*Cf. Gen 2:23

throne as the days of heaven'.* And again, 'I have sworn once by my holiness [I will not lie to David] ; his seed shall remain for ever and his throne as the sun in my sight and as the moon for ever full, and as a faithful witness in heaven.'* I ask you: where is that promise? Where is that throne of David, perfect as the sun in the sight of God and lasting as the days of heaven? But the Truth does not deceive nor is he deceived, especially when blessed Jacob says, 'The scepter shall not be removed from Judah nor the leader from his loins until he that is to be sent shall come and he will be the expectation of the nations.'* Come to the Church of God and you will see the Son and Lord of David sitting on his throne with great power and majesty.

But if you still shamelessly and irrationally contend and say, 'When Christ comes our race will reign with him,' look at the primitive Church sprung from your race. See your brothers, how they reign with Christ. See their hearts live for ever.* Peoples tell of their wisdom and the whole Church of the saints proclaims their praise. Tribes and nations beseech them and the sons of their mother, that is the Church, bow before them. Blush therefore, enemies of Christ, to be trodden beneath the feet of him to whom it was said by the Father, 'Sit on my right hand until I make your enemies your footstool',* and begin to be among his members that you may drink the blood of salvation which your fathers poured out to their own destruction.

And what shall I say concerning you gentiles? You are our flesh and bone.* This makes us more anxious concerning your salvation. Why do you not believe that Christ is God? You believe indeed that he was born and that, being born of the Virgin, he lived without sin. But because you do not believe that he is God, you make a dangerous mistake and sin to your own destruction. But you say, 'We have been taught so to believe by our prophet.' If you wish to know that that prophet of yours was false, we condemn him from his own words and from his own lips reprove his folly. He said that Christ was truly born of the Virgin, that he lived free from falsehood or any sin. But Christ, who according to this testimony was always truthful, claimed openly in the Gospel— prophets and apostles bearing him witness—that he was God and the Son of God. Therefore he was a liar who maintained that Christ was not God.

For refuge therefore betake your very selves to the catholic and apostolic Church; for just as once, in the flood, no place of safety was found but the ark of Noah,* so now there is no place of refuge but the Church of Christ. *Gen 7*

Leaving these matters aside, let us return to our subject and let us weigh carefully the difference between the child-bearing of Mary and that of Eve. Eve bore a child, being corrupt. Mary brought forth, being incorrupt. Eve in pain, Mary in health. Eve in the 'old man', Mary in the new. Eve brought forth a slave, Mary a Lord. Eve a guilty one, Mary a righteous one. Eve a sinner, Mary one who justifies from sin. The childbearing of Eve multiplies deaths, that of Mary saves from death. While Eve gives birth, the dragon lies in wait. At Mary's child-bearing angels minister. Terror of heart seizes upon Eve in labor, but as Mary brings forth divine power gladdens her.

Those, Eve, whom you brought forth you expose to many misfortunes. Your offspring, Mary, you save from all evil. As Eve gave birth, malice abounded, but when Mary did grace superabounded. The heavens were glad, earth exulted when Mary gave birth and hell was troubled and aghast. The heavens in their joy produced a shining star and a glorious army of angels, uttering praise and saying 'Glory to God in the highest and on earth peace to men of good will.'* *Lk 2:14* The earth exulting brought shepherds giving glory and magi adoring and offering gifts, gold, frankin- cence and myrrh.* Hell, disturbed, brought the *Cf. Mt 2:1-11* wicked king and moved to rage his minions to stir them to the slaughter of the innocents, with no pity for the unborn, and killing those they snatched from the breasts.* So at Mary's childbearing the *Mt 2:16-18* good rejoiced, and the wicked were dismayed, for he was being born who would render good things to the good and strike the evil with the vengeance they deserved.

Consider that when the mother gave birth, the face of the universe smiled and the glad world applauded its Lord. Reflect that the clouds were swept away and the sky put on its beauty and the stars, saying 'here we are',* blazed with joy for him. Reflect that night poured forth light in the darkness and instead of blackness offered radiance that night gave light before the sun arose and a brightness which from its exceeding brilliance obscured the splendor of the sun. Concerning this night the psalmist says 'Night is my light in my delights'* and turning to the Lord he follows and says, 'The darkness will not be dark with you and the night will be as bright as the day,'* for his darkness is as his light.

Pleasant and clear shone the warmth of the air and all things in peace bore witness in their order that the author of peace and sweetness had come. Do you not think that at the birth of Christ the whole world was at peace when you read that at his death it was thrown into confusion? Would all things be troubled at his death and not be in peace at his birth? Would they perceive in their senses that he was dying and not know that he was being born?

If all things rejoiced at his birth, how did his mother rejoice? If all things were glad, how great a gladness did she enjoy? What happiness was in the mother if all things were so glad? The tongue falters, the heart fails, the mind is aghast at the weight of a joy so great. For how could so frail a vessel, still made of clay and mortal, hold out before such mighty joys? For at the birth of Christ he overshadowed her who overshadowed her at his conception. He gave her the power to bear the joys, who granted her their wealth, and the strength of his divinity with wondrous power controlled her whom the glory of his majesty filled with unspeakable richness.

When therefore she had brought forth the promised Son and had given birth to the day from day for our day, turning to God with her whole heart she gave voice to her thanks and praise on high, offered

*Bar 3:35

*Ps 139:11

*Ps 139:12

the acceptable sacrifice of her lips and offered the sacrifice of her jubilation,* gave the peaceful holocaust of her heart and for a burnt offering to the Lord sacrificed the sweet perfumed incense.* Taking up the new-born Emmanuel, she beheld a light incomparably fairer than the sun and saw a fire that water cannot quench. She received in the covering of the flesh she had borne the light that lightens all things and she was worthy to carry in her arms the Word that carries the universe. Filled therefore with the knowledge of God as the waters of the sea when they overflow, she is carried outside herself and with heart raised on high she stands still in deepest contemplation. She marvels that she, a virgin, has become a mother and with joy marvels that she is the Mother of God. She knows that in her have been fulfilled the promise of the patriarchs, the oracles of the prophets and the longings of the fathers of old, who foretold that Christ would be born of a virgin and with all their prayers awaited his birth.

Cf. Ps 27:6

Cf. Dt 27:7, Lev 4:31

She sees the Son of God given to her and rejoices that the world's salvation is entrusted to her. She hears him speaking to her and the Lord God saying in her 'Behold I chose you from all flesh* and made you blessed among all women.* See, I have entrusted to you my Son, committed to you my only Son. Fear not to suckle the one you have borne, to train up the one you have brought forth. Know him not only as your Lord but as your Son. He is my Son by his divinity, your son by the humanity he has taken.'

Si 45:4
Lk 1:28

With what feeling and eagerness, with what humility and reverence, with what love and devotion then did she fulfil this task is unknown to men, but known to God, who searches the reins and the heart and who weighs the soul.*

Ps 7:9 & Pr 16:2

Often, as we believe, forgetting to eat and drink, disdaining the needs of the flesh, she spent sleepless nights that she might think in her spirit upon Christ, might see in the flesh Christ from whom she was on fire with longing, whom she was on fire to serve. Often also she did what was written in the Canticles: 'I sleep and my heart keeps watch.'* For asleep in the flesh she was awake in the spirit, dreaming in the

Sg 5:2

quiet of night of him whom day by day she thought upon, waking she found herself in him, and yielding her limbs to slumber she rested sleeping in peace.*

Where her treasure was, there was her heart also.* Where her glory was, there also was her conscience. She loved her Lord and her Son with all her heart, with all her mind, with all her strength, with all her heart,* because with complete affection. With all her mind because with her whole understanding, with all her strength because with the whole purpose of her heart and the carrying out of all his commandments. She saw with her eyes and with her hands handled the Word of life.* Happy she to whom it was given to cherish him who cherishes and nourishes all things, to carry him who carries the universe, to suckle a son who pours milk into the breasts, to feed him who feeds all things and provides food for the birds.*

The Wisdom of the Father clung round her neck and in her arms rested the Power that moves all things.* The little Jesus stood on his mother's lap and in her virgin bosom rested that rest of holy souls.* Sometimes tilting his head while she held him with right hand or left, he bent his gentle gaze upon his mother, he whom angels longed to look upon,* and called her mother with sweet murmur, he whom every spirit calls in time of need.

Filled with the Holy Spirit she clasped the sacred breast of her Son to her own breast and pressed his face to hers. Sometimes she kissed his hands and arms and trustingly, with a mother's privilege, took sweet kisses from his sacred mouth. She was not sated with beholding him nor satisfied with hearing him. Him many kings and prophets desired to see and saw not, and to hear and heard not.*

She progressed further and further in love, and her spirit burning in her ever wakeful soul was fixed upon his divine glances. For love of her Son she feared neither toil nor grief nor dangers nor poverty nor want, neither terrors nor death nor the rage of the wicked king, the flight and return from Egypt. She was most pleasing in her activity, full of joy in what she did, prompt in obedience, devoted in her service,

Cf. Ps 4:8
Mt 6:21

Mt 22:37

Cf. 1 Jn 1:1

Cf. Ps 147:9

Cf. 1 Cor 1:24
Cf. Mt 11:29

1 P 1:12

Lk 10:24

humble in her submission. In everything she acted
with success; she ordered all things vigorously and
wisely. With countenance serene and tranquil mind
she accomplished all the duties of humanity. For as
she was unlike any other in contemplation, so also
in the active life she found no equal.

Where does this discourse lead? We are defeated
and are glad to be defeated. We have attempted
what is far above us, we are lying far below. Let us
therefore return to ourselves and wash away our sins
with weeping. Let us ask the Mother of pity to grant
us, by the hidden joys and unspeakable love which
by unique privilege she earned, the desire for her
motherly love and to plead with her Son for our sins.

At the end of the discourse the reader will know
that four homilies remain in the order in which the
last four steps in the ascent of Blessed Mary have
been put forward. The first will tell the suffering and
the sword which the glorious one endured when
Christ was dying. The second will explain the glory
she felt when he arose. The third will be of her
assumption and exaltation. The fourth will treat of
the fulness of perfection which she will have one day,
we hope with us and from us.

HOMILY V

REMEMBERING our promise and knowing that we can do nothing of ourselves, for we are not in anything sufficient of ourselves,* we pray the Father of lights* to enlighten our hearts and to open our lips.

*2 Cor 3:5
*Jas 1:17

We must know that there are two kinds of martyrdom, the one clearly seen, the other secret; the one hidden; the one in the flesh, the other in the spirit. In the flesh the holy apostles and martyrs suffered. They spent themselves for their love of truth and their witness to Jesus, and having become Christ's victim they drank the cup of the Lord,* that by the cross they might mount to glory and by a death in time they might be worthy to be made partakers of eternal life. It is they who in the Song of Songs climb the palm tree to seize the fruit* and by the crimson ascent are gathered into the litter of the true Solomon, so that they recline on a golden couch and are enriched with delights of every kind,* eating and drinking in the kingdom of God,* Christ ministering to them.

*Cf. Mt 20:22

*Sg 7:8

*Sg 3:10
*Lk 22:30

But those saints suffered in the spirit who in their spirit endured something more cruel than suffering in the flesh. In spirit Abraham suffered when, being bidden to sacrifice his only son Isaac whom he loved, he was deeply moved by his fatherly love and was stirred to the depth of his heart by his affection for his son.* Nevertheless as a diligent workman he performed the task laid upon him and, hastening to obey the divine command, he reached in a three days' journey Mount Horeb. There, as commanded, he put

*Gen 22

together the heap of wood, bound Isaac and laid him
upon it. He seized his knife and would have slain his
son had he not been checked by a voice from heaven
and heard 'Stretch not your hand against the lad. Now
Gen 22:12 I know you fear God.'* That man suffered more than
in the flesh because he did not hesitate to offer in
faith and devotion the son whom he loved more than
his own flesh and finally on that third day showed he
was fully intent upon the deed.

Similarly Moses suffered in the spirit when he
Ps 106:23 stood in the breach before the face of God* and
prepared to pray for the safety of his people. He cast
far away his own safety, saying, 'either drive away
this plague from them or blot me out from the book
Ex 32:31-2 you have written'.* What a dart in the heart! What a
blow inflicted on the very depths of the soul!
'Either drive away this plague from them or blot me
out from the book you have written.' He chose to be
Rom 9:3 anathema, far from Christ, on behalf of his brothers,*
and considering the safety of others his own, he was
more distressed for another's loss than for his own. He
did not believe life would be complete for him if he
lived while others died and if he alone entered the
kingdom while others were in danger. For charity
1 Cor 13:5 seeks not its own,* because it places the common
good before its own, not its own before the common good.

For this reason David too suffered in the spirit
when he saw the angel slaying the people and he
groaned and, turning in his heart to God, he said that
he had sinned and done evil and he prayed that the
2 Sam 24:17 sword might be turned against himself.* He excuses
Israel and demands that he be destroyed, with his
stock, provided that the sword dripping blood might
cease from slaughter and the avenging wrath no
longer destroy the innocent. From these examples,
I think, we see that the martyrdom of the spirit goes
beyond the torments of the flesh.

Therefore the glorious lady [Mary], triumphing in
this kind of suffering, the more glorious as she was
nearer them all, clung to the revered cross of the
Lord's passion, drained the cup, drank the passion

and, having quaffed the torment of grief, was able to
endure a grief unlike any other. She hastens after
Jesus not only for the scent of his perfumes,* but in
the abundance of his sorrows. Not only [does she
follow] for the joy of his consolations but also for the
wealth of his sufferings. His mother perceived the
true Solomon in the diadem with which she had
crowned him* and she, herself crowned with the
crown of affliction, followed after him.

She stood near the cross* that she might see her
son's sweet head anointed with oil above his fellows',* beaten with rods, and crowned with thorns—
heart-rending sight! She saw there was neither form
nor beauty in him who was lovely with a beauty
beyond the sons of men.* She saw him who was high
above all nations despised and of no reputation,* the
holy of holies crucified with criminals and malefactors, the eyes of the lofty man brought low, the
head of the sustainer of all things sagging to his
shoulders, the radiant face of God wither away and
the glory of his countenance hidden.

Therefore to him it was said by the prophet:
'Truly you are a hidden God.'* Why hidden? Because
he had neither form nor beauty,* yet power was in
his hands. There [in his hands] was hidden his
fortitude.* Was he not hidden when he submitted his
hands to things powerful* and his palms received
the nails? The print of the nails gleamed on his hands
and his innocent side received the wound. They
shackled his feet in fetters, the iron pierced his soles*
and his feet were fastened to the tree. These wounds
did God suffer on our behalf at the hands of his own
people, in his own home.

O how marvellous are his wounds, by which the
wounds of the world were healed! How victorious his
wounds, by which he slew death and stung hell.
'Death,' he says, 'I will be your death. I will be your
sting, o hell.'* Leviathan was caught on the hook†
and while he opens his mouth to eat the worm that
cried out in the psalm 'I am a worm and no
man',* he halted, wounded with the iron [sword]
of those wounds. With these precious wounds was the

*Cf. Sg 1:3

*Sg 3:11

*Jn 19:25

*Ps 45:7

*Ps 45:2
*Is 53:2-3

*Is 45:15
*Is 53:2

*Hab 3:4
*Pr 31:19

*Cf. Ps 105:18

*Hos 13:14
†Cf. Job 40:20,
Gregory the Great,
Moralia 33,7;
PL 76:680C

*Ps 22:6

devil snared and man set free.

Therefore, o Church, o dove, you have coverts in the rock and a hollow in the wall in which to rest.* Fear not raging Goliath,* the cruel-hearted, by his countenance uttering mighty threats, since he has been robbed of his strength with his own sword by the true David. He wished to strike and he found a striker. He sought to wound and himself was grievously wounded. He tied himself up in his own knots and was thrown down by his own effort. He seized upon what was not his and lost what belonged to him. He attacked another's and lost his own.

The blood of Christ was weighed in the balance, and in the Father's judgement proving the heavier, it destroyed the sins of men and the devil's chains. Therefore being despoiled alike of his most cherished vessels and of everything in which he boasted and of the weapons in which he trusted, the ancient foe is reserved for the judgement and will pay the penalty for ever for having poured out the blood of the Son of God. And you, ungrateful Jews, blasphemers, parricides, you will burn with him, so that he will have as companions in the fire those whom he found to help him in his crime.

The Lord says, 'I have nourished and raised up sons, but they have contemned and despised me.'* In truth, he nourished and raised you up, and through your wickedness he was raised upon the cross. He clothed you in scarlet in the delights* and beauty of glory, and by your madness he was stripped naked. A glorious crown protected you,* and upon his head you set a crown of thorns. He fed you with the flour of wheat* and to him you gave gall to eat. He says: 'they gave me gall to eat and when I was thirsty they gave me vinegar to drink.'* He lengthened the cords of your inheritance and strengthened the pegs [of your tents],* but you stretched out his arms, and fastened with nails the hands that raised your dead.

At this the sky was aghast and clothed itself with darkness as with a hair shirt. Sun and moon withdrew their light and were surrounded with grief. They were seen to weep for their Creator. The air was blackened

*Sg 2:14
*1 Sam 17

*Is 1:2

*2 Sam 1:24

*Pr 4:9

*Ps 147:14

*Ps 69:21

*Is 54:2

and ringed about with thick darkness. The earth trembled and shook.* Rocks were rent, graves were opened and from hell the dead arose.* Hell itself shuddered at the crime and hell's furies were dismayed. But the Jews, more unfeeling than the earth, harder than the rocks, more cruel than hell, more unbelieving than the demons, neither perceived the Lord nor broke his heart nor shuddered at his crime nor exercised his faith.

And what will you do, o wicked people, sinful race, house that shed the blood of the crucified, when he comes in the clouds with great power and majesty?* He will come down with heaven and earth ablaze, and by the terror of his coming he will dissolve the elements; and when he has come, the sign of the cross will be seen in the sky, and the beloved one will show the scars of his wounds and the prints of the nails by which he was transfixed in his own home.

Then you will weep over yourself, with lamentation as for an only son.* You will say to the mountains 'cover us' and to the hills 'fall upon us'* before the sword of the dove* and before the anger of God's wrath. He will set you in a furnace of fire on the day of his appearing, in his anger he will confound you, and the fire will devour you.* A raging whirlwind will seize you, a fierce tempest will drown you, unending fire will burn you and the chaos of hell will enfold you, as—too late—you offer your prayer. And do not say, as you are wont, 'he prophesies for a distant day'.* Behold, the Lord causes you to be carried away as a barnyard cock is carried off, and he will remove you* like a worn garment†, so that despised and an exile, you will die in a land not your own and, worn out by a double contrition,* you will, through distress alone, regain the knowledge you lost and learn by your punishment what in your sin you presumed upon.

Therefore the heart of the glorious Virgin, burned with unspeakable sorrow equally for the death of her son and the loss of the Jews and pierced with a great dart of pity, sighed in deep anguish. She drained a cup

*Ps 77:18
*Cf. Mt 27:45-52

*Mt 24:30

*Cf. Jer 6:26
*Lk 23:30
*Jer 46:16

*Ps 21:9

*Ezk 12:27

*reading
    sublevabit *for*
    sublevavit
†Is 22:17
*Jer 17:18

more bitter than death itself and that which the human race could not endure, she—a woman—was strong enough to bear, assisted by the grace of God. She overcame her sex, she overcame human nature, and she suffered beyond what was human. She was more tortured than if she was suffering torture in herself, since she loved infinitely more than herself the source of her grief.

And to leave out for a while that bitter grief for the death of her son, who would describe with what sorrow the blessed Virgin was racked, with what anguish pressed, when with the eye of prophecy she saw the condemnation of most of her own race, the blotting out of the nation and the overthrow of the once holy city of Jerusalem? Certainly the prophets, knowing the future, had foretold the destruction of the Jews and with many tears followed their ruin. The Lord himself wept over Jerusalem* and the apostles long mourned their country's treachery. Paul, filled with pity, desired to be ana- thema from Christ for the sake of his brethren according to the flesh,* that he might rouse them to their salvation and to emulation. How much more would the mother of pity do everything, willingly bear everything, expose herself to whatever pains, even to death, that she might remove from her race the destruction and disaster that threatened it. But the king's honor loves justice* and the undeniable justice of the high God most justly arranged that over which the gracious mother of the Redeemer wept in her pity.

Let no one argue that the Jews were hateful to the Mother of God for their having condemned her Son to a most shameful death. For those whom she saw near to eternal death she in no way considered to deserve her hatred and insult, but to deserve great affection, many tears, and a great pity. Therefore sharing in the charity as well as in the cross of Jesus, she took up her prayer for them and with her whole heart, beating on the ears of the Father's pity, said, 'Father, forgive them this sin, for they do not know what they are doing'.* This, his utterance, was her

*Lk 19:41

*Rom 9:3

*Ps 99:4

*Lk 23:34

desire, that the more effectively the ears of the unconfined spirit who fills and hears all things everywhere might be beaten upon.

For the rest, whoever you are who love the Mother of God, take note and reflect with all your innermost feelings [upon her] who wept for the Only-begotten as he died, and on what was demanded of her. The grief she felt in the passion of her son goes beyond all understanding, goes beyond man's comprehension. No simile, no comparison comes near such bitter grief.

For what mother loved her son as she did? Not by chance did she, like other women, conceive him, but the only Son of the Father entered his mother's womb by loving choice and free bounty. This is why she loved him more. Nor did he bring, as others do, any pain to his mother in his life, but he poured upon her abundance of grace, as the Scripture says of him: 'He did no sin nor was guile found in his mouth.'*   *1 Pet 2:22 Again, concerning grace: 'Handsome with a loveliness beyond the sons of men, grace has been poured upon your lips, because God has blessed you for ever.'* This is why she loved him more. She had the   *Ps 45:2 same son as God, for he was born in her as man, and the All Highest himself established him. This is why she loved him the more incomparably. For she alone from eternity was worthy to have as son him who was also God.

Therefore, with deep calling to deep,* two loves   *Ps 42:7 had come together into one and from the two loves was made a single love when the Virgin mother gave to her Son the love she gave to God and showed her love for her son in loving God. Therefore the more she loved, the more she grieved and the greatness of her love brought the increase of her suffering.

What was she doing when she stood on Calvary and saw the cross, the nails, the wounds of the One who was dying in innocency and the insatiable cruelty of the Pharisee afire with malice? He [Jesus] hung there atoning not for his sins but for ours, and the Pharisees with the Scribes, mocking him, struck him on the head and offered to his lips vinegar mingled

*Jn 19:29

*Ps 69:26

*Cf. Is 13:8

with gall*—that there might be fulfilled the prophecy of David, saying in the person of Christ, 'They added to the pain of my wounds.'* In the midst of this the Mother of God was distressed in mind and sorrows seized upon her as upon a woman in childbirth.* There are groans, sobs, sighs, sorrow, grief, agony, distress of heart, fires, a death more cruel than death. There life is not taken away yet the bitterness of death is suffered. O memory to be revered, full of devotion and tears, to recall how that glorious holy soul suffered, and what anguish she endured in the death of Christ. The pale face of Jesus reflected the bloodless face of his mother. He suffered in the flesh, she in her heart. Finally the insults and scoffing of the wicked came back upon his mother's head. The Lord's death was to her more bitter than her own [would have been]. Although, taught by the Spirit, she would not doubt the resurrection, yet she had to drink the Father's cup* and to know the hour of her own passion. Concerning this, the venerable Simeon prophesied to her: 'A sword shall pierce your soul.'* O Lord Jesus, terrible in your counsels beyond the sons of men,* you did not spare your mother from the sword piercing her soul.* By this road must we all pass by the fiery sword turning this way and that to the tree of life which is in the midst of paradise.*

*Cf. Jn 18:11

*Lk 2:35

*Ps 66:5
*Ps 105:18

*Gen 3:24

But to return: Blessed Mary was able to cry out that which was especially appropriate to Christ: 'O all you who pass by, behold and see if there is any sorrow like my sorrow.'* What a sorrow and how great! And in that sorrow what was Mary like? Alas, as she was then, how different from the girl who had once tended her son amid a choir of angels while shepherds worshipped and Magi adored him with an offering of mystic gifts. Very different, not indeed in virtue but in sadness, not in grace but in grief. For she increased in virtue and grew in grace. For set in the midst of adversity she neither relaxed her modesty nor lost the strength of her constancy.

*Lam 1:12

*De obitu
Valentiniani
consolatio
39; PL 16:
1431D

For proof of this, blessed Ambrose, bishop of Milan, says of her: 'I read of her standing by the Lord's cross, but I read not of her weeping.'* For to

stand in such bitterness of heart is ascribable to her
mighty constancy; to abstain from tears is the mark
of the utmost self-control. She held back her tears
from modesty, she stood there from a certain loftiness
of soul. Therefore grief did not draw tears from her
nor pain overthrow her spirit. For on the one side
a befitting modesty, on the other a valiant constancy contended.

Therefore, beloved, let us imitate the Lord's
mother so that in the midst of adversity we do not
forget reserve and we remember constancy. Griefs
will not be lacking, adversities will not be lacking,
temptations will not be lacking, and death itself will
make its way through us. Let us fortify our soul with
humble reserve and firm constancy. Let our reserve
continue in death and our constancy of spirit persist
amid swords. Then being made by the likeness of
our character like to the Mother of God, we shall be
brought after her into the temple of the King,*   *Ps 45:15
through the same Christ our Lord.

HOMILY VI

EAT, MY FRIENDS, drink and be inebriated, beloved.* I invite you to the table of wisdom and to libations of wine which she [wisdom] has mixed for you* in the bowl. I invite you to the banquet of the glorious lady, to the feast of the Mother of God. Happy he who, received at such a banquet, shall shine forth in the marriage garment amidst the guests.* The bread of life will be set before him, strengthening, filling, satisfying him with its wondrous sweetness, and the wine of gladness, the wine coming forth from the fruit of the vine, truly the wine of the resurrection pressed from the tree of the Lord's passion. This wine that grape produced which, brought from the promised land, hung upon the bar of wood.

More, the aforesaid guest will eat, clad in a fine robe and wearing the ring of peace, after the fatted calf has been slain by the Father.* [He will eat] with his loins girt with the girdle of faith and chastity, having also shoes on his feet,* as being prepared for every good work,* and he will eat the flesh of the Paschal Lamb roasted with fire.* Nor will there be wanting, if the guest wishes, the fawn of a pleasant roe* and a stag leaping upon perfumed mountains, a leaping from the valley of hell to the mount of heaven.* Next, after taking the fish which was found near the sea shore above the plum trees,* when the Lord appeared to the disciples in the resurrection, he will at the same time taste the honey comb.* And taking the song of the Song of Songs, he will say on that day: 'I ate the comb with my honey. I drank my

*Sg 5:1

*Pr 9:5

*Cf. Mt 22:11

*Cf. Lk 15:22

*Ex 12:11
*2 Tim 3:17
*Ex 12:8

*Cf. Pr 5:19

*Cf. Sg 2:8
*Cf. Jn 21:9-10

*Cf. Lk 24:42

109

*Sg 5:1
*Sg 8:5

*Sg 5:1

*Cf. Bernard, Dil
XI, 32-3; CF 13;
123-5

*Qo 3:4

*Mal 4:2

*Cf. Jn 10:9

*Ps 21:1-3

*Source unknown

wine with my milk.'* Abounding then in every
delight* he will invite others with him to the feast,
saying, 'Eat, my friends, drink and be inebriated,
beloved.'*

I, too, brothers, invite you to this feast. Eat,
drink, and be inebriated, beloved. Eat the bread of
life, drink the wine of gladness, be inebriated with
the joy of the resurrection. This inebriation is the
height of sobriety.* It blots out remembrance of the
world and always stamps upon the mind the thought
of God's presence. Everyone drunk with this forgets
all things and remembers only the charity of God.
Therefore, be you also drunken, beloved, be drunken
along with the Mother of God and rejoice. Rejoice in
her joy, you who have mourned with her grief.

Solomon says there is a time for joy and a time for
grief.* Grief has departed, the time for joy has come,
that true joy which proceeds from Christ's resurrection. For he has risen and he has raised up his
mother's soul. She lay as in a narrow tomb of grief
while the Lord lay in the sepulchre. As he arose, her
spirit lived again and, waking as if from deep slumber,
she saw in the morning light the sun of justice* and
the rays of his rising. She gazed upon the beginning of
the rising dawn and the future resurrection of her
flesh, coming before time in her son. She feasted her
eyes upon the glowing flesh of the risen Lord and in
her heart perceived the glory of his godhead, so that
within and without, leaving and entering, she enjoyed
the pasturage of true and everlasting felicity.* Beside
herself, therefore, forgetting self for joy, she clung
with all her heart to the Father of spirits and bound
fast to God she poured out upon him her whole self
and was wholly flooded in the immensity of his love.

Lord, in your strength she rejoiced greatly and she
will exult mightily in your saving help. You have
granted her her heart's desire and not withheld from
her the request of her life, since you have anticipated
her with sweet blessings. You have placed on her
head a crown of precious stone.* The crown of her
head is Christ because, as the wise man says, a wise
son is his mother's crown.* And who is wiser than

he who is the Father's wisdom? It is rightly called a crown of stone because in the New Testament Christ is meant by the word 'stone'.* He was called stone because of his power, precious because of his glory. The psalmist, combining the two, says briefly, 'The Lord of hosts, he is the King of glory.'* Because he is Lord of hosts, he is therefore a stone. Because he is the king of glory, precious. Truly nothing is stronger than stone, nothing more precious than glory.

 *Cf. Mt 21:42, Ps 118:22

 *Ps 24:10

Therefore, O blessed one, you possess your joy. Your desire is fulfilled and Christ, your crown, has brought you through grace the sovereignty of heaven, through pity the kingdom of the world, through vengeance the submission of hell. For you the victor rose from hell, he wore down the gates of brass and broke the bars of iron.* He occupied hell's fortresses and crushed the dragon's head. He inflicted great slaughter upon his enemies and bound the prince of hell. He slew death and cast into chains the author of death. That author of death was bound with chains of fire.

 *Ps 107:16

Then he brought back his own from the darkness and broke their chains. He united with himself the souls of all the just, walking in the light of his countenance and rejoicing in his name.* Raised high by his justice are they who were brought low through injustice. The Lord Jesus was alone in his journey to hell, as David sang, saying for him: 'I am alone until I pass over.'* Alone as he entered but by no means alone as he went forth, for he brought back with him countless thousands of the saints. He fell to the earth and died that he might bear much fruit.* He laid himself down at seed time that he might at the harvest gather the human race.

 *Ps 89:15-16

 *Ps 141:10

 *Cf. Jn 12:24-5

Happy the womb of Mary in whom that seed took root. Happy she to whom it was said, 'your womb is like a heap of wheat set about with lilies.'* Was her womb not like a heap of wheat which swelled with that grain from which the whole harvest of the twice-born has grown? For at the baptismal font, dead to the sins within ourselves, we are born again

 *Sg 7:2

Cf. 2 Cor 5:15
Tit 3:5

Gal 3:27

to Christ* through the cleansing of regenera-
tion,* that we may live to him who died for all. So
the Apostle says, 'as many of you as were baptized
in Christ have put on Christ.'* Therefore from one
grain come many harvests and that grain [came] from
the virgin's womb. It is called a 'heap' from the
power, not the number, of the seeds; from its
strength, not its multiplicity.

It is said to be hedged about with lilies because the
everlasting inviolability of the mother's womb is
proved by the holy sayings of Scripture. What are the
divine utterances but lilies diffusing the whiteness of
purity and breathing a pleasing odor of sweetness?
For this reason the Word and Wisdom of the Father is

Wis 7:26

called the brightness of eternal light.* And concerning
the holy utterances, the psalmist says: 'The words of
the Lord are pure, silver tried in the fire, tested in the

Ps 12:6

earth, seven times purified.'*

Concerning its perfume, it is written in the
Canticle: 'We will run toward the perfume of your

Sg 1:3

unguents.'* It is the voice of young maidens rejoicing
in the fragrance of the bridegroom's words. 'We will
run towards the perfume of your unguents', that is,
to the knowledge of your utterances. For the
utterances of the Lord are precious unguents, by
which the sickness of souls is driven out and by which
is applied the medicine appropriate to the wounds.
By these antidotes the dread poisons of the serpent
are scattered, to their warmth the cruel wounds
yield, by their help is cured that wounded man who

Cf. Lk 10:30ff

went down from Jerusalem to Jericho.* Again concerning their perfume, in the same Canticle, this is the
voice of the Bridegroom to the bride: 'The

Sg 4:10

fragrance of your unguents surpasses all perfumes.'*
In another place he says, 'Your breasts are better

Ibid.
†*Sg 1:2*

than wine,* more fragrant than the best perfumes.'†

The Church, the bride of Christ, has the breasts of
the Testaments by which she pours the milk of
consolation on her little ones, and on the full-grown

*Cf. William, Cant
40; CF 6:36-7,
Bernard, SC 10:2;
CF 4:62*

the milk of exhortation.* It is no marvel the
full-grown are nourished on her milk, for she says,
'I am a wall and my breasts are like a tower,

therefore I have become in his presence as one seeking peace.'*

   These breasts are said to be better than wine, for Paul bears witness: 'The foolishness of God is wiser than men.'* Better therefore are her breasts than the wine of empty philosophy, than the wine of earthly knowledge, than the wine of worldly greed, not indeed a wine pressed from the vineyard of Sorek* nor of Cyprus, nor the vineyard of Engedi,* but from the vineyard of Sodom and the outskirts of Gomorrha, or at least from the grapes of gall and the fruit of bitterness.*

   Therefore young maidens, mindful of the bride's breasts, long to be nourished with an abundance of that milk rather than wine, that by it they may increase in health. 'Better are you breasts than wine fragrant with the choicest perfumes.'*

   These breasts are fragrant with the choicest perfumes, since the aforesaid Testaments of the Church become known by their perfect utterances, so that in proportion to their ability to comprehend, some they feed with a veneer of history, others they teach by moral beauty, others they raise on high by their mystic meaning.* They are also fragrant with the choicest perfumes when to the same Testaments is added the grace of spiritual discernment and the virtue of divine charity, so that like certain lilies they shine white with the gift of discernment and are perfumed with the sweetness of love.

   Among these lilies the beloved feeds, as the voice of his beloved says: 'My beloved,' she says, 'is mine and I am his, and he feeds among the lilies.'* He feeds among the lilies when the soul of the one who reads in the Scripture is satisfied with the inner sweetness of his word. Surrounded then by those lilies the Mother of God hears from the lips of Solomon, 'Your belly is as a heap of grain surrounded with lilies'.*

   The souls of the saints can also be understood as lilies, gleaming white through the merit of their life, fragrant through their example. Of the whiteness the psalmist says to God: 'You shall purge me with hyssop and I shall be clean. You shall wash me and I

*Sg 8:10

*1 Cor 1:25

*Cf. Jg 16:5
*Sg 1:14

*Dt 32:32

*Sg 1:1-2

*On the levels of Scripture, see Cassian, Conf. 14,8 (forthcoming CS 20)

*Sg 2:16

*Sg 7:2

Ps 51:7
Ps 45:1

2 Cor 2:14-15

Phil 4:1

shall be whiter than snow.'* Concerning the perfume
he says: 'My heart has uttered a good word.'* The
Apostle also: 'We are the good perfume of Christ to
God in every place.'* Surrounded therefore by the
lilies of the redeemed, the Mother of the Redeemer
will most fittingly be able to say this word so appropriate to them: 'My joy and my crown.'* You have all
been gained by blood derived from my blood and by
flesh taken from my flesh.

With these lilies also was he hedged about when he
snatched the souls of the just from hell and blessed
them with the riches of his glory. The true Jacob
crossed the Jordan of mortality on the staff of the

Cf. Gen 32:10

cross and returned with two squadrons.* I understand
the two squadrons as circumcision and uncircumcision,
those who were under the Law and before the Law.
Therefore he died alone and lived again with great increase. For as in Adam all die, so in Christ shall all be

1 Cor 15:22

made alive.* By his death we have been increased, by
his blood our root has grown up, by his resurrection
our body has lived.

He has flowered not as grass but as the Word, not
as days of the world but as the days of heaven. Hence
by the voice of the Father it is said concerning the
seed of David: 'I will establish his seed for ever and his

Ps 89:29
Is 11:1

throne as the days of heaven.'* Therefore an everlasting flower has sprung up from the root of Jesse;* it
was dried up by the passion but it flowered again at
the resurrection. It flowered again, not to wither
later like the flower of the field, but to remain the

Is 40:8
Jn 1:14

Word of God for ever.* For the Word was made flesh
and dwelt among us.* For that reason Daniel, a man
of longings, said that the Son of man came to the
ancient of days that he might show himself son of

Dn 9:23

man.* Seeing this the psalmist rightly says, 'Your
throne, O God, is for ever and ever. The sceptre of
righteousness is the sceptre of your kingdom. You
have loved righteousness and hated iniquity. Therefore God, your God, has anointed you with the oil of

Ps 45:6-7

gladness above your fellows.'* Look at him whom
God names, whose seat, he says, is for ever and ever.
After this he says that this one was anointed by

God with the oil of gladness above his fellows. For
being God from eternity, he reigns with the Father
for ever, and as man in time is anointed with the oil
of gladness above his fellows. He was truly above his
fellows, for the Father says to him: 'You are my son.
This day have I begotten you.'* And that saying: 'Sir   *Ps 2:7*
on my right hand until I make your enemies your
footstool.'* That you may know that he is equal to   *Ps 110:1*
the Father as touching his divinity, hear him say in
the Gospel: 'I and the Father are one',* and 'He who   *Jn 10:30*
sees me sees also the Father.'*   *Jn 14:9*

Of him also the Apostle says: 'Therefore God has
exalted him and given him a name above every name,
that at the name of Jesus, every knee should bow, of
things in heaven, things on earth, and of things under
the earth.'* In truth, the knee of those in hell bends   *Ph 2:9-10*
before him in dread, the knee of those on earth
through self-interest, of those in heaven through their
blessedness. On the first he inflicts punishment, the
second he brings out from their wretchedness, the
third he raises in glory. To the first he is terrible in
judgement, to the second pitiful in aiding them, to
the third generous in rewarding them. He subdues the
demons with his sword, redeeming men with his
blood, satisfying the angels with the sight of his
countenance. Therefore hell bends the knee, trembling
at his power; earth bows the knee, praising his mercy.
Heaven bends the knee crying out 'Holy, Lord God of
hosts. Heaven and earth are full of his glory.'*   *Is 6:3*

He himself is your son, O Mary, he himself rose
from the dead on the third day and with your flesh
ascended above all the heavens that he might fill all
things. Therefore, O blessed lady, you have your joy,
the object of your desire and the crown of your
head have been granted you. He has brought to you
the sovereignty of heaven through his glory, the kingdom of the world through his mercy, the subjugation
of hell through his power. All things with their
diverse feelings respond to your great and unspeakable glory: angels by honor, men by love, demons by
terror. For you are venerated in heaven, loved in the
world, feared in hell.

Rejoice therefore and be glad, for he who receives you has arisen, your glory, lifting up your head.* You rejoiced at his conception, you were afflicted at his passion. Rejoice again in his resurrection and your joy no one will take from you.* Christ, rising from the dead, dies no more. Death will have no more dominion over him.* The spirit calls you, God says to you: 'Arise, hasten, my love, my dove, my fair one and come. For the winter is past, the rain has departed and gone, the flowers have appeared on our earth. The time for pruning has come.'*

*Ps 3:3

*Jn 16:22

*Rom 6:9

*Sg 2:10-12

My love by wedlock, my dove by union, my fair one through your beauty and elegance. Rise up from grief, from affliction, from humiliation and out of the dust, which are the marks of sorrow. Hasten, away with delay, shake off your burden, put off your heaviness, put on lightness, run, take wing, and come. Come that you who lately grieved may rejoice, come that you may see the glory of God, the first fruits of the resurrection, the first born from the dead.* Now the winter is past in which Peter, benumbed, denied, in which the frozen hearts of the Jews extinguished for themselves the sun of justice,* having kindled the embers of their passions. The rain is over and gone, the stormy downpour, bringing mud, bringing ruin, mingled with snow and hail, it is over and gone. The rain of those who cried out and said: 'Crucify, crucify him'* is over and gone. Gone too the rain by which the Gentiles' threshing floor was deemed worthy to be watered, while the fleece of the Jewish people was dried up.*

*Cf. Col 1:18

*Cf. Mal 4:2

*Jn 19:6

*Cf. Jg 6:40

Flowers have appeared in our land, flowers everywhere of blessed spirits and of angels blooming in alternation and sprinkling the place where the Lord has been laid with sweet perfume. These the Old Testament set forth in symbol when above the mercy seat at either end it set up two carven cherubim or painted them with palms on the doors of the tabernacle.* The meaning is clear: hidden then in symbols, now revealed in reality. Palms bear the sign of the resurrection. The doors and the mercy seat point to him who is the open door to the kingdom

*Cf. Ex 37:7-9, 1 K 6:29

and the propitiation for the sins of men.* The two
cherubim are the two angels who sat one at the head
and one at the feet where the body of Christ had
been laid.*

They are rightly called flowers because the eternity of the high God gives them an eternal spring so
that they always bloom, never wither, never fall, and
remain the same with their beauty untouched. Flowers
also appeared in our land when, as the Lord ascended, two men stood by the apostles, and said to
them, 'Men of Galilee, why do you marvel as you gaze
into heaven? This Jesus who has been taken from
you will come, just as you have seen him go
into heaven.'*

The time for pruning has come. Hell has been
pruned and the devil has been cut off from the heart
of the believer. The mouth of the Lord has separated
the precious from the worthless,* cutting the dead
twigs from the vines and gathering the darnel from
out of the harvest, that he may heap the grain into
the barns, throwing the weeds on the pyre to be
burnt.*

O unhappy separation! Grief and joy everywhere
intermingled. O sweet and bitter day, when the
righteous judge, returning from hell, on some turned
his back, to others showed the face they longed for.
Some he abandoned for punishment, others he raised
as joint heirs in his kingdom. The former he sent
away to burn with the devil,* the latter he carried
with him to be crowned in heaven. The wicked saw it
and groaned in hopelessness. The good saw it and
rejoiced with all their heart.

O wretched ones whom mercy did not aid! O
blessed ones, to whom it came in glory. O wicked
ones whom even the passion of the Only-begotten did
not help. O happy ones, whom it rescued from
eternal death. The wicked saw and groaned in hopelessness. The good saw and together lifted up their
voice in triumph.

And you, glorious lady, saw your Son rising from
hell. You saw with your blessed eyes your son's
glory. You saw and you fainted. Your flesh and your

*1 Jn 2:2

*Jn 20:12

*Ac 1:11

*Jer 15:19

*Cf. Mt 13:30

*Cf. Mt 25:41

*Ps 73:26
*Sg 5:6
heart failed.* You turned to water when you heard
the voice of your beloved* son speaking to you. His
word became like a fire burning in your bones. Therefore inflamed by the divine words you became wholly
like a fire and you offered yourself as a sweet sacrifice
to God. O phoenix, sending forth perfume more
Cf. Si 24:20 pleasing than cinnamon and balsam, sweeter than
nard delighting the king by its presence. O phoenix,
gathering together all chosen beauties, surrounded
by supersubstantial fire, that you may fill the heaven
of heavens and the angelic powers of heaven with a
wondrous sweet incense. This incense is most sweet,
this well-compounded frankincense comes forth from
the censer of Mary's heart and sweetly surpasses
Cf. Ex 30:34-8 every perfume.

Then the censer following the incense and lifted
up by the hand of the Lord mounts to the throne of
God. It goes up attended by a train of angelic spirits
calling out on high and saying, 'who is this who comes
up through the desert like a column of smoke from
the odor of myrrh and incense and all the powders
Sg 3:6 of the perfume?'

But now let our discourse [now] brought as far as
the ascension be brought to an end, so that with God's
help another may more fully describe this ascension.
Amen.

HOMILY VII

AS I REFLECT and often ponder over in my mind the assumption of the Mother of God, a certain question comes to my mind, worthy of examination, profitable when answered, which will obviously be pleasant when it is shared. The question is why, when the Lord ascended into heaven, did his mother who embraced him with such affection not follow him at once? Since she was weighed down with no cloud of sin, soiled with no spot on her life, glowed more than a fire because of her charity, was brighter than the light by reason of her chastity, even outdistanced the denizens of heaven through the uniqueness of the virgin birth, it seemed strange that she was not carried at once to heaven with her Son.

Doubtless Enoch walked with God in purity of heart and was seen no more, for God took him.* Elijah also, burning with the great fire of charity, is said to have been carried away by a chariot of fire and horses of fire.* But she who surpassed Enoch in purity of heart and was greater than Elijah through the privilege of her love, why was she not straightway carried into heaven along with him whom she bore? For she was full of grace and blessed among women.* She alone was found worthy to conceive true God from true God.* She, a virgin, bore him. She, a virgin, gave him suck, cherishing him in her arms, in all ways she served him with the reverence of an underling. Finally she suffered with him in his death, more in mind than in body. She lived again in the Spirit in his resurrection, and why did she not ascend with him in his ascension? Her sacred flesh

*Gen 5:24

*2 K 2:11

*Lk 1:28
*Cf. Nicene Creed

which was pregnant by the Holy Spirit, which swelled by the seed of the mighty King, in which God *Jn 1:14 was made man and the Word became flesh,* and by the mediation of Christ the fulness of his divinity *Col 2:9 remained in her bodily,* [that flesh] would seem meet to be brought to heaven when the Lord was taken up. Why was she held back even for a moment? Why did she suffer separation from her Son? Why was her holy desire, hotter than fire, held back?

Because that delay was no small comfort for Christ's disciples. That delay did not detract from the mother and it brought to the world the medicines of salvation. For the Lord Jesus willed that on his return to his Father his disciples should enjoy maternal comfort and teaching. Though indeed they had been taught by the Spirit, yet they could be taught by her who put forth to the world the sun of *Cf. Mal 4:2 righteousness* and brought for us from a virgin meadow, from an unspotted womb, the fount of *Cf. Si 1:5 wisdom.* In short, with wondrous goodness provision was made for the primitive Church which no longer saw God present in the flesh, that it might see his mother and be refreshed by the lovely sight.

For what is there so lovely, so seemly and delightful, as to behold the mother of the Creator and Redeemer of the world? If the sepulchre of that same Redeemer, which still exists today, is so delightful in our sight, if the stone on which rested the holy stock *Cf. Is 11:1 of Jesse* is sought out by such a great concourse that it calls forth the affections and thoughts of all men and attracts everything by a kind of religious charm, what joy was it to see the Mother of God as long as the divine pity allowed her to stay with us on earth in our common life?

Ps 33:12 Blessed nation and happy generation which was worthy to be enlightened with such a sight. Blessed indeed the generation in whose midst, believing and rejoicing, stood the tree producing the life-giving *Cf. Gen 3:3,22 fruit.* The mother of the true light shone forth, and there was seen that well, closed and sealed, from which issued the spring of the house of David, open *Zec 13:1 for the washing away of sin and defilement.* This unique privilege, this heavenly gift, this special grace was offered to the primitive Church.

Finally the virgin Mother granted a share in all the gifts of grace within her. For as soon as she was seen glowing with the fire of holy love, she sweetly inflamed the hearts of those near her, brought faith to the hearts, urged them to modesty, made what was honorable lovely, drawing them to righteousness. She breathed the flower of virginity, sowed the untilled field of chastity, portraying before their eyes the picture of humility and showing them the mark of truthfulness. Around her was an unfailing brightness and in her face a glowing fire.* A swift-flowing river of fire went forth from her* to set on fire her foes, to warm her friends, to help her neighbors, to burn up her enemies. It is said by those who understand the nature of living things that the poisonous snake by the mere sight of it and by its deadly breath kills whatever is near it. In the same way she, hotly inflamed by its nearness with the heat of the divine fire and sprinkled with the blazing flames of the Word, breathed forth the scent of the grace of the resurrection upon those who were far off and those who were near.* *Cf. Ps 18:8* *Dan 7:10* *Is 57:19*

Indeed for some, that is those against her, it was the odor of death into death, but for others who believed in her Son the odor of life into life.* For as in Eve all die, so in Mary will all be made alive.* And as by the sin of Eve comes the condemnation of the world, so by Mary's faith has come to pass the world's restoration. The one [Eve] was infected with a deadly poison which she handed on to her posterity. The other [Mary] was filled with a life-giving antidote which she transmitted to all the faithful. The one fell, mistakenly trusting the serpent; the other rose up and, according to the word which in Genesis God had before spoken, bruised the serpent's head,* having been foretold from the beginning and now presented to the primitive Church, once promised and now revealed at the end of the age. *Cf. 2 Cor 2:16* *Cf. 1 Cor 15:22* *Gen 3:15*

Who would not hasten, who would not run from the ends of the earth to gaze upon the beauty of the venerable majesty and to behold the countenance endowed with all manner of sweetness and with commanding dignity and unique power? Indeed, nothing was found like to her among the sons and daughters of Adam, none such among the prophets, apostles or angels. Heaven and earth have put forth nothing like her. Who in the clouds would equal her* or be like the Mother of the Lord among the sons of God?

*Cf. Ps 89:6

And see how fittingly before her assumption her wonderful name blazed forth in the whole world and her renown was everywhere spread abroad before her grandeur was raised above the heavens.* For it was fitting that the Virgin Mother, for the honor of her Son, should reign first upon earth and then, at last, receive the heavens with glory, should tarry in the depths that she might enter the heights in the fulness of sanctity; and just as she was carried from virtue to virtue so by the Spirit of the Lord be borne from esteem to esteem.*

*Cf. Ps 8:1

*2 Cor 3:18

Therefore while present in the flesh she tasted in advance the first-fruits of the future kingdom, now going forth to God in unspeakable sublimity, now in wondrous charity condescending to her neighbors. On the one side she was attended by the services of angels, on the other venerated by the devotion of man. Gabriel, the groomsman, with the angels was at her side; John, with the apostles, ministered to her, rejoicing that at the cross the Virgin Mother was entrusted to him.* These [the angels] rejoiced to see their queen; those [the apostles] to see their lady, and all obeyed her with pious devotion.

*Jn 19:27

But she, dwelling in the lofty citadel of the virtues and enriched by an ocean of divine gifts, poured out in generous diffusion upon a believing and thirsting people an abyss of graces, in which she surpassed all others. She brought health to their bodies and cure to their souls, being powerful to raise them from the death of body and soul. Who ever went away from her sick or sad and not knowing heavenly mysteries? Who did not return to his home glad and joyful, having obtained from the Mother of God his wish?

The presence of Mary brought the sweet warmth of spring, and wherever she turned with her favor was paradise. 'Your plants,' said the Spouse, 'are an orchard of pomegranates and apples: cypress oil with nard, nard and saffron, calamus and cinnamon, with all the trees of Lebanon, myrrh and aloes, with all the chief spices, a fountain for gardens, a well of living waters and swift streams from Lebanon.'* For **Sg 4:13-15* the garden of the glorious lady has pomegranates in the variety of her virtues, pleasant fruits in the perfection of her works. She has also cypress-oil with nard, the one heavy with grapes, the other a fragrant herb with wondrous odor, because of the sober intoxication of her senses and the sweet and fragrant esteem of her virtues. To these are added the saffron of gladness, the calamus of the ravaging of the flesh, the cinnamon of sweet gentleness, with all the trees of Lebanon by which is typified the sum total of all her virtues. The myrrh of mortification and the aloes of incorruption, with all the chief perfumes, poured out without loss of that perfume which poured upon the head and came down to the beard, Aaron's beard;* not the Aaron of old, who was the type, but **Ps 133:2* the new one, the typified. And it came down to the hem of his garment,* which is the Church, presented— **Ibid.* as Paul says—to that true Aaron without spot of wrinkle.* The bride therefore, enriched with these **Eph 5:27* great gifts, mother of only bridegroom, sweet and beloved for her charms, as a spring in spiritual gardens and as a well of living and life-giving waters which flow swiftly from the divine Lebanon,* distri- **Sg 4:15* buted from Mount Sion to all the peoples round about rivers of peace and the overflowings of grace poured out from heaven.* **Cf. Is 66:12*

Blessed David, speaking of his son our Lord, says: 'There will be in his day righteousness and abundance of peace'; then presently speaking of her he rightly added: 'until the moon be taken away'.* She is **Ps 72:7* indeed the moon which lighting up the heavens and the earth shines far brighter than the stars (that is, the saints), 'until,' he says, 'the moon be taken away'; the moon which when the sun of righteousness arose stayed in its own place and first shone forth upon the primitive Church.

The faith of our ancestors according to true history relates that from the birth of the Saviour to the passing of the glorious lady the world's inhabitants rested in calm unbroken peace, the madness of war being stilled. These things we have said in answer to the question set before us, that we might show with what advantage the death of the mother of our King was postponed.

Indeed, we must mark also how from this postponement every faithful soul, wounded with charity, pierced with the darts of love, learns not to complain that it does not go hence in answer to its prayers. Look, the Mother of the Lord suffers delay, who would dare to murmur? She suffers delay that she may advance, she advances through her perseverance. Perseverance, joined to love and work, creates fulness, brings forth perfection. Hence comes what is rightly spoken by the voice of the psalmist: 'the righteous will flower as the palm tree, as the cedar of Lebanon will he be multiplied.'* The palm is said to flower after a long space of time and the cedar of Lebanon multiplies after a long passage of years. So the righteous, as his soul grows white with age, will flower like the palm with the long lapse of time. The said psalmist aptly added a few words: 'They will still be multiplying in ripe old age.'* We should then note that Mary, endowed with surpassing merit and unique righteousness, who was worthy to be exalted above the angels, had first to be multiplied here in a fruitful old age. When this came to pass by God's gift, her hidden being and the beauty which she wore in secret (having become brighter than light and surpassing every loveliness) turned towards her the faces and hearts of the citizens above with wondrous love.

But now, who would worthily extol her holy assumption? Who unfold in words how joyfully she went forth from the body, how joyfully she beheld her Son, how exultingly she hastened to the Lord, attended by choirs of angels, supported by the reverence of apostles, while she beheld the King in

*Ps 92:12

*Ps 92:14

his beauty* and saw her Son awaiting her with glory,   *Is 33:17
free from every ill as she was free from all corruption?
She was brought forth from the house of her flesh to
live for ever with Christ. She passed over in the vision
of God, she breathed out to God her blessed soul,
brighter than the sun, higher than the heavens, of
more worth than the angels. For by her glorious passing is lit up Mount Sion, where at the end of her days
she passed away in happy old age. It was there that
she completed the last service of her life, giving full
and perfect fulfilment of all her virtues. There the
armies of God hasten to meet her rising not dying,
departing not dying, and the heavenly hosts hasten
to meet her.

How precious in the sight of God is his mother's
death!* What life will equal her death? What joy her   *Cf. Ps 116:15
passing? You may bring together earthly loves, feasts
and triumphal banquets, everything that sweetens
and delights the whole world, yet this [death] is
lovelier and sweeter than them all. For it is a libera-
tion from the flesh, a road to life involving no pain,
no bitterness, no terror. In place of pain, it cherishes;
instead of bitterness it delights; and in place of terror
it strengthens the faith of the one who stands on the
shore. It brings no darkness, for it reveals eternal
light. It does not take away life for it directs to the
author of life.

By this death the glorious lady departed, if we
may call a passing into life 'death'. Rather, to speak
truly, life is where death alone dies, where the body
of death is shed, where the life of the flesh now departed in a holy rest is preserved for the time to come
with manifest gains. Is it not life when one goes to
the source of life and drinks eternal life from life in
an unbroken stream? Of this unfailing draught the
virgin Mother tasted even before her death, so that
in her very passing she should not be touched by the
slightest taste of death. Therefore as she went forth
she saw life, that she might not see death. She saw her
Son that she might not grieve at her separation from
the flesh. Therefore going out free with such a happy
vision and being possessed of the face of God that she

had longed for, she found the revered citizens of
heaven ready to render service and attend her.

They marvel that this soul of unique merit, freed
from the everlasting taint of sin had not a spot of the
flesh or of the world. They marvel that, freed from
the body, she glowed with the grace of perfect purity.
What should they first praise in her: integrity or
humility, prudence or charity, vigor of mind or for-
bearance, the honor of her motherhood or the
novelty of the birth? But yet more praised in her is
her perfect virtue and fulness of grace.

Therefore the Lord, present at her departure
from the body, thus proclaims her prasies: '*You are
all lovely,* my mother, *and there is no spot in you.*
You are all lovely, he says,* lovely in thought,
lovely in word, lovely in deed, lovely from your
beginning to your end, lovely in the virgin conception, lovely in the divine birth, lovely in the crimson
of my passion, lovely in the brightness of my
glorious resurrection. *Arise, therefore, my beloved,*
my dove, my fair one, my spotless one, *and come, for*
the winter of my absence *is past, the rain* of your
tears *has departed and gone* and with the sun's
return, angelic *flowers appear* for you. Your *voice,*
chaste dove, *has been heard. The time* of your
assumption *has come.*'*

Therefore when the Virgin of virgins was led by
God and his Son, the King of kings, amid angels
triumphant, archangels rejoicing and heaven resound-
ing with praises, there was fulfilled the prophecy of
David saying to the Lord: 'The queen stood on your
right hand in vesture of gold wrought about with
divers colors.'* Then according to the word of
Solomon: 'Daughters have risen up and called her
blessed and queens alike have praised her.'* 'Who is
she,' says the heavenly virtues, 'who ascends in white,
leaning upon her beloved?'* And again: 'Who is she
who goes forth like the rising dawn, fair as the moon,
choice as the sun?'* Again they said: 'Who is she who
goes up through the desert like a column of smoke
from perfumes of myrrh and incense and all the
powders of the perfumers?'* That splendor is for us

*Sg 4:7

*Sg 2:10-12

*Ps 45:9

*Cf. Pr 31:28

*Cf. Sg 8:5

*Cf. Sg 6:9

*Sg 3:6

strange and wondrous, strange and glorious, this plan of her assumption, strange and pleasing this most sweet odor.

Escorted amid such praises, she herself could not refrain from praising, for she saw the Son of God, born of her, sitting on the right hand of his Father's majesty, receiving her with glory. 'You have held,' she says, 'my right hand, and have led me according to your will and received me with glory'.* And again: 'He is at my right hand lest I be moved. Therefore my heart has rejoiced and my tongue has exulted. Still more my flesh shall rest in hope. Since you did not abandon me in the world nor did you give your Mother's body to see corruption.'*

*Ps 73:23-4

*Cf. Ps 16:8-10

But why do I linger over these things? To sum up much in a few words: there was with the most glorious lady a word simple yet complex, a word understandable, containing all the words of praise with which she herself honored the Lord and Son with praise unutterable.

Exalted therefore with cries of exultation and praise, she is placed in her seat of glory first after God, above all the company of heaven. There, having taken again the substance of her flesh (for it is not lawful to believe that her body saw corruption) and clothed with a double robe,* she looks upon God and man in his two natures with a gaze clearer than all others, inasmuch as it is more burning than all, with the eyes of her soul and body.

*Cf. Pr 31:21

Then coming down to the human race in ineffable charity and turning upon us those eyes of pity* with which heaven is brightened, she lifts her prayer alike for clergy, for the people of either sex, for the living and for the departed. Here from heaven is the glorious Virgin most powerful in prayer, driving away every hurtful thing and bestowing what is good, and she grants to all who pray to her from the heart her protection for this present life and for that to come.

*Cf. Salve Regina hymn

For remembering for what purpose she was made the Mother of the Redeemer, most willingly she gathers up the sinner's prayers and pleads with her Son for all the guilt of those who are penitent. Surely

she will gain what she wishes, the dear Mother
through whose chaste womb the Word of God came
to us, the sin offering of the world, to wash away with
his own blood the bond of original sin, Jesus Christ
Our Lord, who lives and reigns with God the Father
in the unity of the Holy Spirit, God for ever and ever.
Amen.

HOMILY VIII

S EVERAL DAYS, beloved, have passed in which, under the burden of the episcopate and encumbered with great anxieties, I have been unable to provide for your holy hunger the promised meal concerning the praise of blessed Mary. Now therefore, if the blessed Virgin favors me, I will not fail you, withdrawing myself indeed a little from my affairs but inclining to your pious wishes.

Therefore let us with unremitting duty do honor to the Queen of Heaven, Mother of Life, Fount of Pity, abounding in charm and resting upon her Beloved,* **Cf. Sg 8:5* and let us laud her—though our praise be inadequate. Let us in spirit be raised on high, noting carefully that the beauteous rod sprang from the root of Jesse* by **Is 11:1* the marvellous spreading of its branches stretched over the whole world,* that with welcome shade it **Cf. Ps 80:11* might protect the scattered sons of Adam from heat, from tempest and from rain, and nourish the hungry with health-giving fruit. Towering therefore over all the trees of paradise and raised above the lofty summits of the highest mountains, she, in her unbelievable greatness, entered heaven itself, attended by the choirs of the heavenly orders and honored by the dances of virgins.

O the splendor, glory and magnificence of this tree by whose never-failing fruit, by whose undying nourishment there is provided a perpetual feast for the inhabitants of heaven and earth, an unbroken rejoicing, a blissful and never-ending praise. Blessed are they who eat meat in your kingdom.* Blessed are **Cf. Lk 14:15* they who dwell, O Lord, in your house. For ever

*Ps 84:4
and ever will they praise you.* In you also shall be
praised not Eve, who gave death to drink, but Mary,
giver of life, mother and nurse of all men, life of the
*Gen 3:20
living.* In you shall your mother be praised.
*Ps 34:2
*Cf. Is 14:12
Let the gentle hear and rejoice.* Lucifer the
boastful has been wounded and falls to the depths.*
Let the proud hear and be brought low. The humble
virgin is crowned and mounts to the throne of glory.
Let the humble hear and be glad. He has fallen, he
that was raised on high by his great presumption.
*Cf. Ps 66:33
Mary has entered among the burnt offerings* by
yielding herself wholly to the fulness of grace. He,
hardened with ill will, will never proceed to rise
*Ps 41:8
*Cf. Ps 62:2
again.* She, strengthened by charity, will never be
so shaken as to fall.* For clinging with unshakeable
firmness to the immovable centre, she could never be
disturbed by any changeableness. He, going beyond
the noble bounds of angelic dignity, striving after that
which a created spirit does not approach, pursuing a
mere void, rushes over steep places, is shrouded in a
dark horror, sliding down to the depths of the pit to
grieve eternally and to pay the penalty in the torments
of a just damnation.

He who is rightly named the devil, that is, 'falling
*Isidore of Seville,
Etymologiarum
8. 11. 18; PL
82:316A
backwards'*(because he disappeared from the heights,
envying those who stood firm), he plunged with himself into the depths those whom he could. He
prompted those who trusted him to seek for honors,
position, superiority, to savor what is lofty, to lift
*Ps 75:5
their horn on high,* to love the applause of the
crowd, greetings in the marketplace, the first seats at
*Cf. Mt 23:7
gatherings,* to scorn their inferiors, to put themselves
before their equals, to envy their betters, to forget the
glory of God, to bring under their sway some by
flattery, others by threats or torture, to set themselves up as idols, to do all things to be seen of men
and to be praised.

When he has raised to the clouds these wretched
ones, proud, puffed up, amazed and demented, then
finally he turns the same ones, cruelly enfeebled,
towards all that is shameful and dishonorable; and
when they are so turned he hurls them, along with

himself, without pity into the depths of hell.

But the glorious Virgin, with flesh untouched and tranquil mind, gentlest of the living, the lowlier and holier she is than all others, the higher was she raised above all and she was received into heaven by its citizens with every mark of honor and in the fashion of a queen and was bidden by the Supreme Father to sit down in the kingdom of eternal brightness and on the throne of surpassing glory, first in rank after the Son whom she bore incarnate.

Mighty God, terrible and strong,* of unspeakable goodness, you raise and exalt your humble handmaid to the place from which you had long ago driven out your jealous foe, so that humility might triumph, adorned by you with the increase of grace and a glorious crown,* yet pride, empty and dark, might fall in ruin. *Cf. Neh 1:5* *Pr 4:9*

Conspicuous therefore by her unparalleled merit the blessed lady stands before the face of her Creator interceding always for us with her powerful prayer.* Taught by that light to which all things are bare and open,* she sees all our dangers, and our merciful and sweet lady pities us with motherly affection. *Cf. Heb 7:25* *Heb 4:13*

The holy creatures of which one reads in Ezekiel that they are full of eyes before and behind, within and without and round about,* cannot weigh as can the Mother of God the toils of men, their griefs, misfortunes, failures, blindness, weaknesses, deadly perils, the uncertain end of life and every ill of the human race and, by weighing them, with heaven's help dispense and drive them away. The more she beholds from on high the heart of the mighty king the more profoundly she knows, by the grace of divine pity, how to pity the unhappy and to help the afflicted. *Ezk 1:18*

So she was called Mary, that is, star of the sea, in the foreseeing purpose of God, that she might declare by her name that which she manifests more clearly in reality.* For from the time she ascended to the heavens to reign with her Son, robed in beauty, robed equally in strength, she has girded herself, ready to curb with a single gesture the extraordinary *Cf. Bernard, Miss II.17*

*Ps 92:1,4
tumults of the sea.* For those who sail upon the sea of the present age and call upon her with complete faith she rescues from the breath of the storm and the raging of the winds and brings them, rejoicing with her, to the shore of their happy country. One cannot tell, beloved, how often some would have struck hard rocks, about to suffer shipwreck, some fall on foul sandbanks to return no more, some the whirlpool

*See Aeneid III.
432, 684, V. 122

*Ibid. V. 864
Scylla would have engulfed in its fearsome depth,* some the Siren's sweet songs would detain to their destruction,* did not the star of the sea, Mary ever virgin, stand in the way with her mighty aid and when now the rudder was broken, the deck shattered, and they were without human aid, bring them by her heavenly leading to the haven of inner peace.

Therefore rejoicing in new triumphs in the new rescue of the boat, in the new additions of peoples, she manifests her joy in the Lord and, not content with spoils she has won but eager for man's salvation, the malicious foe driven further and further away, she is always winning more and more trophies. So with

*Ps 136:12
powerful hand and arm upraised* she advances into the tyrant's realms, attacks all the strongholds of the demons, making hell tremble beneath her feet and the prince of death shrink back, struck with a mighty dis-

*Jb 40:10
may. Finally, at her bidding Behemoth* spews forth the prey which he had made to pass into his malicious belly, casting out with regret that which he held in his inordinate arrogance. The fallen arise, the penitent

*Ps 112:10

*See above,
Hom V, p. 101

*Ps 112:10
return. The sinner will see and will rage.* His jaw, pierced with the hook of the Saviour's cross,* gives back as freedom those whom before he held captive, gnashing his teeth and wasting away.* Through the Mother they are reconciled to the Son, through the Virgin they are reconciled to God, being given back to life, utterly withdrawn from death.

The desire of sinners will perish, but the desire of blessed Mary is fulfilled when every day those in chains are led forth from the pit of sorrow and its

*Ps 40:2
muddy dregs,* so that from the prison-house of sin and the depths of iniquity they may breathe, by the gift of pardon, the air of everlasting freedom. Thus

she gathers together those who were scattered, she calls back the wanderers, rescuing those being led to death. And those whom she sees being dragged to torment she ceases not to set at liberty. Not only for the salvation of their souls but also for the health of men's bodies she takes thought and heals them, and with duteous care takes thought for their needs. In the places dedicated to her holy memory she wins movement for the lame, sight for the blind, hearing for the deaf, speech for the dumb,* curing every kind   *Cf. Mt 11:5 of weakness and affording countless gifts of healing.

There come to her doors men beating their breasts, confessing their sins, and having received pardon they return home with joy. There come also those who are sick in mind, weak in the head, the mad, the maniacs, the possessed, those who are led astray by nightly terrors, by some phantasma or by a genuine attack of the evil one, and they regain their health and receive the generosity of the divine gift. In the same way there draw near to her feet those whose hearts are bitter: the sad, the needy, the afflicted, the lonely, those tied up by debt and, most grievous of all, those living in dishonor and besmirched with the stain of ill-repute.

The prayers of all these who cry out of whatever tribulation she gladly receives and, making supplication to her Son, in her pity she turns from them every evil. For just as wax melts at the touch of fire and as ice melts in the heat of the sun, so the army of her foes perishes before her face and at her bidding nothing hostile stands.

But we must mark and carefully consider with what love, with what great kindness she embraces and loves those who are akin to her in purity of heart, she who, as has often been said, by her intercession constantly frees from the death of sin and from eternal pains worthless and wicked men. Indeed, glowing and conspicuous with this twofold love on the one hand, she is most ardently fixed upon God to whom she clings and she is one spirit with him;* on   *Cf. 1 Cor 6:17 the other she gently comforts and attracts the hearts of the elect and shares with them excellent gifts

coming from the generosity of her Son. Therefore
with her swift motion outstripping the winged

*Cf. Is 6:2

seraphim,* now at the fount of life she enjoys the love
of the Godhead, now lighting up the world with her
miracles and powers she everywhere succours her own
as a joyful, openhanded mother.

Some men her presence makes conquerors by sub-
duing their vices, some by her kindly intercession she
makes possessors of great virtues; to certain ones she
reveals the secret of interior contemplation, to others
at their end she shows the sure road, so that no
might of the enemy dismays those whom the Mother
of the Only-begotten God guides to Christ.

There are very many examples of what has been
said which we shall for the sake of brevity omit as
being generally well-known. But you must know for
certain that frequent miracles, countless benefits,
spiritual visions, heavenly revelations, lofty consolations of the gentle Mother of the Lord will constantly shine forth in the world until the world itself
grows old and finds its end, as dawns the Kingdom of

*Lk 1:33

which there is no end.*

But meanwhile there comes to mind that notable
day of judgement whose greatness the holy prophet

*Cf. Ps 56:4

David declared he fears,* and which all the faithful
always know to be approaching. In that moment of
awful examination the King of heaven will be present
with his holy mother, attended by angels and archangels and the whole army of the heavenly host to
judge the world in righteousness and its inhabitants

*Ps 98:9

with justice.*

Then will she shine forth in glorious light, she
through whose virgin womb and closed door God the
king of glory shone upon the world. Then will be
revealed the truth of patriarchs and prophets who
witnessed aforetime to the god-bringing childbearing
of the Virgin. Her Son's apostles, imitators and witnesses of her virtues, will also bring to her glory and
honor, for illuminated by his teaching and strengthened by the spirit of wisdom that fell upon them
from heaven, they have filled the Church with the
splendor of the true sun.

Martyrs will rejoice, seeing the glorious lady whom on earth they loved, whose merits while life lasted they celebrated with their praise. They will rejoice, I say, gazing on that unique diadem which on that day of solemnity and joy, the day of her assumption and glory, Christ placed upon the head of his beloved mother, calling to mind the crown with which she had crowned him on the day of the betrothal.* *Sg 3:11*

Virgins will run in the scent of her perfumes,* *Sg 1:3* hastening to enter with her into the wedding that, joined with her for ever in the heavenly marriage chamber to their true spouse, they may sing, with Mary leading the new song* which no one can utter *Rev 14:3* unless he be virgin in spirit and body. Lastly each sex, every age, every rank and every honor will call her most blessed and a people beyond counting will cry out to her in jubilation, being saved by her merits and prayers and crowned at his right hand by the good Lord.

May it be our good fortune to be in their number and in their fellowship, o tender, o sweet Mary, so that when the day of wrath comes, the day of tribulation and of grief,* we may not be punished for our *Zeph 1:15* sin, but through you, Lady, we may be deemed worthy of his mercy who ascended to the Father to prepare a place* for his servants that he might set *Jn 14:2* them in the lovely country of heaven, in the bright resting places of paradise, amid the sparkling fiery stones of Jesus Christ our Lord, whose is the splendor, honor, power, glory and greatness
with the same Father and the Holy
Spirit, through infinite
ages of ages.
Amen.

INDEX

INDEX

St Bernard: *In Praise of the Virgin Mother*
(Arabic numerals refer to paragraph numbers)

INDEX OF PERSONS

Amadeus of Lausanne, *Homilies on the Praises of the Blessed Mary*
(Arabic numerals refer to pages)

INDEX OF PERSONS

Aaron
  I 66; VII 123
Abraham
  I 64; III 85; 86; IV 87; V 99
Adam
  I 63, 64; III 82; IV 88, 90;
  VII 122
Ambrose of Milan
  V 106
Apostle, The
  I 62, 66; II 74; VI 114, 115.
  See also Paul

Behemoth
  VIII 132

Christ
  passim
  Author of peace and sweetness
    IV 94
  Blessed fruit of Mary
    III 82
  Bridegroom
    I 64; II 71-2; III 84
  Brightness of eternal light
    VI 112
  Creator
    V 102
  Emmanuel
    I 64; IV 95
  God made man
    I 64
  Good Lord
    VIII 135

Hand of God
  IV 88
Hidden God
  V 101
Incarnate Word
  I 67. *See also* Word
Jesus
  I 65; IV 96; V 99, 101,
  104, 106; VI 117
King
  of glory
    VI 110; VIII 134
  of heaven
    VIII 134
  of kings
    VII 126
  of saints
    I 66
Leader from Israel
  I 63
Lord
  passim
Lord Jesus
  V 106; VII 120
Messiah
  IV 91
New Aaron
  VII 123
Only begotten
  I 65; III 80; IV 88; V 105;
  VI 117
Paschal Lamb
  VI 109
Phoenix

ABBREVIATIONS

ASOC   *Analecta Sacri Ordinis Cisterciensis / Analecta Cisterciensis.* Rome, 1945–

Bern   The Works of Bernard of Clairvaux

  Dil   *Liber de diligendo deo (On Loving God)*

  Miss   *Homilia super missus est in laudibus Virginis Matris (Homilies in Praise of the Virgin Mother)*

  SC   *Sermo super Cantica canticorum (Sermon on the Song of Songs)*

CF   Cistercian Fathers Series. Cistercian Publications.

Conf.   The Conferences of John Cassian

CS   Cistercian Studies Series. Cistercian Publications

Hom   Homily

PL   J.P. Migne, *Patrologiae cursus completus, series latina.* 221 volumes. Paris, 1844–64.

SBOp   *Sancti Bernardi Opera,* edd. J. Leclercq, H. M. Rochais, C. H. Talbot. Rome, 1957–

William   The Works of William of St Thierry

  Cant   *Expositio super Cantica canticorum (Exposition on the Song of Songs)*

Scriptural quotations have been translated directly from the Latin and cited according to the enumeration and nomenclature of the Jerusalem Bible.

CISTERCIAN PUBLICATIONS

Titles Listing

1979

THE CISTERCIAN FATHERS SERIES

THE WORKS OF BERNARD OF CLAIRVAUX

THE WORKS OF WILLIAM OF ST THIERRY

THE WORKS OF AELRED OF RIEVAULX

THE WORKS OF GUERRIC OF IGNY

OTHER CISTERCIAN WRITERS

THE CISTERCIAN STUDIES SERIES

EARLY MONASTIC TEXTS

MONASTIC STUDIES

CISTERCIAN STUDIES

BY DOM JEAN LECLERCQ

DATE DUE

SEP 30 '98			
JAN 1 2 2002			
JAN 0 6 2003			
APR 0 1 2004			